EBURY PRESS
FALLOUT

Salman Masood is a Pakistani journalist who has been working as a Pakistan correspondent for the *New York Times* since 2003. He is also the editor of the Pakistani newspaper *Nation* since 2020, having previously acted as the paper's editor in Islamabad from 2014 to 2020. The focus of Masood's reporting has been on politics, international relations and terrorism. In 2009, he contributed to the *New York Times* reporting team that won the Pulitzer Prize for coverage of Pakistan and Afghanistan.

His writings have also appeared in several other local and international news publications. In 2013–2014, he acted as the editor of *Pique*, an Islamabad-based political and lifestyle magazine. He wrote for the Abu Dhabi-based newspaper *National* from 2008 to 2011. He has appeared as an analyst and guest speaker on the New York Times Public Radio, CNN, BBC and several Pakistani news television networks.

Masood lives in Islamabad, Pakistan.

ADVANCE PRAISE FOR THE BOOK

'Salman, as a seasoned reporter and editor, documents a critical phase of Pakistan's turbulent politics. Sharply written with clarity, this book is a useful guide for scholars, students and general public alike'—Raza Rumi, director, Park Center for Independent Media, Ithaca College, New York

'Salman's lucid eye on the intricacies of politics in Pakistan forms the backbone of this gripping tale that he has written with precision and eloquence. His work is a masterly account of some of the more tumultuous years in Pakistan's recent history, all told in the dispassionate voice of a seasoned journalist'—Kavita Mokha, news editor, *Politico Europe*

Fallout

Power, Intrigue and Political Upheaval in Pakistan

SALMAN MASOOD

EBURY
PRESS

An imprint of Penguin Random House

EBURY PRESS

Ebury Press is an imprint of the Penguin Random House group of companies
whose addresses can be found at global.penguinrandomhouse.com

Published by Penguin Random House India Pvt. Ltd
4th Floor, Capital Tower 1, MG Road,
Gurugram 122 002, Haryana, India

First published in Ebury Press by Penguin Random House India 2024

Dawn leaks illustrations: Saadia Gardezi

10 9 8 7 6 5 4 3 2 1

ISBN 9780143465966

Typeset in Adobe Calson Pro by MAP Systems, Bengaluru, India
Printed at Gopsons papers Pvt. Ltd., Noida.

www.penguin.co.in

MIX
Paper from
responsible sources
FSC® C191020

Power, too, possesses a remarkable ability to win hearts and minds.
—Anonymous

And when you lose control, you'll reap the harvest you have sown.
—'Animals', Pink Floyd

Contents

Introduction   xi
Prologue   xv

Section I (2014–2018)

Chapter 1: All on One Page?   3
Chapter 2: Khan's Gauntlet   6
Chapter 3: A General State of Dysfunction   9
Chapter 4: Government Running Out of Fuel and Ideas   18
Chapter 5: Status Quo   21
Chapter 6: Recapping the Ides of March   24
Chapter 7: The Politics of Vanity   28
Chapter 8: Political Theatre   31
Chapter 9: *Dawn* Leaks: The Who's Who   36
Chapter 10: The Message   47
Chapter 11: The New Army Chief   51
Chapter 12: The Army Chief's Vow: Coordination,
            Not Competition, with Civilians   54
Chapter 13: Imran's Colourful Ally   57
Chapter 14: A New Military Operation   60
Chapter 15: Panama Papers Court Verdict   63
Chapter 16: Opposition Smells Blood in Water   66

Chapter 17: Army Chief and Prime Minister Defuse a
          Lingering Crisis   69
Chapter 18: Last Eid with 'Prime Minister' Nawaz Sharif? 73
Chapter 19: The Contractor   76
Chapter 20: Supreme Court Fires Nawaz Sharif   79
Chapter 21: The Final Round   83
Chapter 22: Nawaz Prepares for a Return   86
Chapter 23: Election Day: 2018 Elections to Change
          Pakistan Like Never Before   90

Section II (2018–2022)

Chapter 24: Come the Revolution   95
Chapter 25: A Unique Prime Minister   98
Chapter 26: A Presidential System Down the Horizon   103
Chapter 27: Prime Minister Khan's Angry Moment   106
Chapter 28: Shambolic Governance and
          Economic Meltdown   110
Chapter 29: Gen. Bajwa Gets a One-Term Extension   114
Chapter 30: Maulana Fazal-ur-Rehman's Game Plan   117
Chapter 31: The Penitence of PML–N   120
Chapter 32: Fawad Chaudhry's Gamble   123
Chapter 33: Sharif's Latest Push   127
Chapter 34: Official Leaks   130
Chapter 35: Imran Meets Trump   133
Chapter 36: The Countdown Begins   137
Chapter 37: The Enigma of Usman Buzdar   141
Chapter 38: Senate 2021: Countdown Begins   144
Chapter 39: The Celebrity Twitter Civil Servant   148

Chapter 40: Gathering Storm 152
Chapter 41: The Fall of Kabul 156
Chapter 42: Civil–Military Divide 159
Chapter 43: Talking with the Taliban 162
Chapter 44: Status Quo or Change 165

Section III (2022–2024)

Chapter 45: The Cipher Mystery 171
Chapter 46: DG ISI, the Intelligence Chief, Steps
    into the Picture 176
Chapter 47: Imran and the Military 179
Chapter 48: General Bajwa: From Benefactor to Pariah 182
Chapter 49: Double Game 188
Chapter 50: General Musharraf: A Deep but
    Controversial Imprint 192
Chapter 51: From Praise to Blame 195
Chapter 52: Mystery about Jinnah House Attack 199
Chapter 53: Political Turmoil Reaches a Crescendo 202
Chapter 54: On the Brink 206
Chapter 55: A Moment of Reckoning for Khan's
    Political Party 210
Chapter 56: Major Shake-Up in Pakistan's Military 214
Chapter 57: Fallout 218
Chapter 58: Bomb, Bulldoze and Destroy 224
Chapter 59: Surprise, Surprise 231

Acknowledgements 237

Introduction

This book, *Fallout*, charts Imran Khan's journey from a combative opposition leader to the office of the prime minister. A crucial element of this commentary lies in the exploration of the complex relationship between Imran Khan and the Pakistani military, and their subsequent falling out. Imran Khan's political showdown since his removal from office after a 2022 parliament vote of no confidence is still ongoing.

The book comprises three sections, each based on my opinion and news analysis pieces published in the Pakistani press from 2014 to 2023. Certain pieces featured in this book were published in the *Nation* newspaper's opinion section, while others were placed in a column called 'The Periscope' on either the front or the back page. The Periscope comprised news analysis articles aimed at forecasting and offering political insights. These pieces have been further edited and updated for clarity and analyse the motives, impacts and undercurrents that have shaped Pakistan's trajectory during these turbulent years.

As a result, there may be variations in the writing style throughout the book. Nevertheless, I hope that readers enjoy the entirety of this book and find it useful in understanding the complexity of Pakistani politics.

The chronological order of events shows how crises steadily escalated during the initial periods of Nawaz's and Imran's governments and eventually led to their removal from power.

Pakistani politics is a familiar tableau where the script remains the same, but the cast keeps changing.

The first section of the book sketches the journey of former prime minister Nawaz Sharif from 2014 to 2017 and details how the Panama Papers scandal paved the way for Imran Khan's rise to power. Sharif initially sought a military alliance, but much like his previous tenures in the 1990s, he eventually found himself at odds with it.

The controversial personality of former army chief General Qamar Javed Bajwa is examined in detail. The book delves into his two distinct roles—one as a professed advocate of civilian supremacy as he initially presented himself, and two, as the creator of the so-called Hybrid Project or Hybrid Rule, a venture that eventually fell apart and led to his disgrace and downfall.

Looking back at an article I wrote in 2017 in *Nation*, I am struck by how my scepticism, shared by some other analysts, seems prescient now. I had written during the Panama Papers scandal, an uproar that many predicted would mark the end of Nawaz Sharif's rule.

However, what was unclear at that time—and which seems apparent today—was the ability of any institutional mechanisms to rise and tackle the deeply entrenched systemic corruption and governance issues. I had posed a question then: would the ensuing struggle ignite a fresh era of accountability and transparency, or would it merely push the country further into the murkiness of power tussles and covert intrigues?

Such an outcome would indeed have sullied the year-long struggle since the Panama Papers revelations, much like the 2007 Lawyers' Movement, which, though successful in restoring Iftikhar Muhammad Chaudhry as the chief justice of the Supreme Court and the eventual removal of military dictator

General Pervez Musharraf, fell woefully short in fulfilling its other pledges of reform and transformation.

As it turned out, the political strife and power struggle that I was concerned about indeed risked—and sadly realized—a similar fate.

Moreover, the decision-making process within both civil and military leadership continues to be inconsistent, intensely personalized and frequently arbitrary. This unpredictability has resulted in the nation staggering haphazardly from one crisis to the next. The absence of institutional stability and consistent policy implementation has exacerbated the myriad challenges the country faces.

Prologue

How Imran and His Benefactors Fell Apart

April 2022

The perception- and image-building effort of portraying Imran Khan as the political messiah originally started in 2011. Some viewed the exercise as filled with noble intentions. There was exasperation with dynasty politics and shambolic governance. Corruption had gnawed deep into the system. There was a need for a reset.

Khan, despite being a political presence since 1996, struggled to make a substantial impact on the established political order. But he had it all: charisma, a clean image, grand promises of reform and earnest-sounding talking points. All he needed was a little push. The public already adored Khan, the country's only global celebrity, who stood tall, handsome and distinct from his peers. But the inertia and resistance to change were much more complex and deeply entrenched. The effort gained momentum in 2013–2014, but it was not until 2018 that '*Tabdeeli*', or change, the political slogan of Khan and his backers in the security establishment, saw its triumph.

A hybrid government was put into place after a lot of pushing and shoving, and its architects saw it as a long-term project. Sometimes also referred to as The Project, it was to last for the next ten years, gradually transitioning the country towards a presidential system of governance. Nothing could go wrong, the architects thought. Already, the past decade of image-building exercises had cemented the narrative about Khan as above the fray in the 'hearts and minds' of most living in urban upper- and middle-class neighbourhoods. High on self-righteousness and full of revulsion for civilian traditional politics, they were deeply invested in the hybrid regime in many ways. A new political order tasted power for the first time. It was intoxicating.

But the beginning was hobbled. The inexperienced lot fumbled and faltered. Khan's lofty rhetoric and promise of principled politics descended into Machiavellian ways. Allies were shunned and treated with scorn. The inner circle grew immensely powerful and unaccountable, untouchable and not to be spoken about. Khan started to enjoy the pomp, show and accoutrements that come with state protocol and privilege. The charismatic sportsman-turned-politician, who could tap into and voice the anguish and disgruntlement of the 'silent majority', vanished. A gaping disconnect emerged.

The cosmopolitan star had, in fact, long disappeared. Now, a new identity was being carved, built on the edifice of conservatism and religious pontification. Khan was now to be addressed with hushed, dutiful tones of reverence. His swagger became more pronounced, surrounded by the men in uniform. And he was now encircled by a coterie of flatterers, uncouth and foul-mouthed, with no local stakes. He liked, approved and encouraged their unhinged ways. Political vendettas eclipsed everything else. Propaganda was touted as a success. Positive criticism was treated as a sign of enmity. The urge to suppress and repress political opposition and the news media became overwhelming and blinding.

During all this time, the Establishment provided unprecedented support. All kinds of tools were used to ensure the new set-up withstood any pressure. But the internal contradictions began to surface soon. The superficial understanding of governance and foreign-policy issues, and an equally amateurish way of dealing with delicate matters of the state began to tear the structure apart. The architects saw through the charade with dismay and shock. Their chosen one was just interested in self-preservation and self-glorification.

The image of one man, larger than life and bigger than everything else, was beginning to weigh down everything. On both internal and external fronts, the incendiary, self-immolating rhetoric was nothing but an illustration of a scorched-earth policy. Arrogance and hubris defined the leader's way of conducting himself. Even the minions and the sidekicks acted with extreme arrogance and dismissiveness. And, most alarmingly, the leader was willing to trample over and shred into pieces the very core of the Establishment that had brought him to the fore.

The disengagement came with a lot of reluctance. In fact, neutrality in the political arena had become a compulsion. But it carried risks and was fraught with unintended consequences.

The ceded space provided the political Old Guard with a big playing field. They took full advantage of it through a successful vote of no confidence in Parliament against Imran Khan. But in the eyes of the public, the political Old Guard was discredited and tainted with long-standing allegations of corruption and malfeasance. Khan, with all his shortcomings and failures, was still better than those who had been dubbed and tarred as incorrigibly corrupt and decadent. It left many within the military, judiciary and civil bureaucracy deeply conflicted.

Khan himself would not go down without a fight. He played the 'conspiracy card' masterfully and turned the game on its head by refusing to play by the rules.

Many mid-ranking and senior military retirees found it exceedingly difficult to pivot to the new reality. The sudden slipping away of power and influence made them angry and frustrated. Understandably, the unexpected crumbling of a ten-year project after 2018 resulted in a meltdown and shock. They took aim at the top brass and were joined in the chorus by a deluge of invective and abuse on social media.

After all, the loyalists were adept at amplifying their voice, using social-media platforms, and creating magical optical illusions. The internal grumbling grew louder. There was talk of a rift. There was a suggestion of dissent within the ranks. Such rumours were deliberately fuelled. Exert enough pressure so it cracks. Pepper with threats initially veiled but with enough intent to show that the gloves can be taken off.

It was brazen. It was also unprecedented. Never have the authority and legitimacy of the most powerful in the land, the top brass, been questioned like this. It also posed a dilemma as a response was calibrated and thought out. The errant insiders could be made to fall in line using the vast coercive apparatus at their disposal. But there is a downside: the more you exercise power, the more it gets diluted. And using it on your own would further widen the fissures. The game of nerves was set to test who would blink first.

The Project collapsed spectacularly. The unravelling happened at a dizzying speed. Its debris is now full of stench and acrid grime. It is a stark reflection of everyone who partook in the power game.

Section I

(2014–2018)

The Build-Up: Nawaz Sharif's Tenure, Panama Papers Verdict, and Imran's Agitational Politics

Chapter 1

All on One Page?

March 2014

The echoes of concern reverberated through the corridors of power in Islamabad as the government's political and military elite gathered for a high-stakes meeting. Their mission: to assess the internal security landscape of the nation. The meeting, held at the Prime Minister's House, stretched over four hours and cantered on the delicate issue of future talks between Taliban negotiators and government officials.

Amidst the discussions on the strategy for peace talks, military and intelligence officials provided briefings on the volatile law and order situation, highlighting the myriad of insurgent groups operating within the country's borders. Terrorism loomed large, posing a grave existential threat that demanded urgent attention. In the past, the state's response to these daunting challenges had been lacklustre, lacking a centralized, comprehensive security strategy. Instead, the government had resorted to reactive firefighting whenever the need arose.

To his credit, the current prime minister, Nawaz Sharif, had taken initial steps to confront the spectre of terrorism, despite facing criticism for his emphasis on exploring peace talks and hesitancy to employ full-fledged force against those challenging the state's authority. Sharif, a seasoned politician with the mind of an entrepreneur, prioritized stability and peace more than anything else. His foremost concern was the potential backlash in Punjab, his political stronghold, and Karachi, the economic nerve centre, where even a spark could ignite uncontrollable violence, given a large number of the Pashtun population, once a military campaign was launched in North Waziristan.

Undeterred by the naysayers, Sharif pursued his strategy of peace talks, acknowledging the fragmented and disjointed nature of the process. A shrewd political move, his visit to Imran Khan's residence aimed to neutralize the most vocal opposition leader, under the guise of cooperation and inclusion. Alongside rallying disparate opposition figures, Sharif sought to address the gaps in existing laws governing terrorism and rectify the dysfunction between various entities within the civil and military security apparatus. Against this backdrop, the meeting at the Prime Minister's Office held particular significance. Prime Minister Sharif evaluated the situation following the implementation of the Protection of Pakistan Ordinance, which faced criticism from certain rights groups. He urged provincial leaders to utilize the strengthened provisions of the law, empowering security forces in both field operations and the judicial process.

Sharif also issued directives to streamline intelligence agencies, consolidating their inputs under the National Intelligence Directorate. Unlike the ill-fated attempt by the Pakistan People's Party (PPP) to bring the intelligence agency Inter-Services Intelligence Directorate, or the ISI, under the Interior Ministry, the Sharif government aimed to avoid such confrontation. As the meeting concluded, Chaudhry Nisar Ali Khan, the interior minister, emphasized that civilian and military leadership were aligned, demonstrating a united front. The issue of civil–military imbalance, a persistent concern in the nation's tumultuous political history, cast a shadow of uncertainty. Despite public assurances of harmony between the two entities on national and international matters, the ongoing treason trial of former military ruler Gen. Pervez Musharraf remained a divisive issue, further clouding the equation.

In the quest for a united front, the government sought to ensure that all stakeholders were on the same page, acknowledging the gravity of the security challenges and working towards a comprehensive strategy. The journey to consolidate and synchronize efforts between the civil and military leadership would be a delicate dance, where the stakes were high, and the nation's stability hung in the balance.

Chapter 2

Khan's Gauntlet

June 2014

Imran Khan, the formidable opponent of the Sharif government, cast his challenge, setting the stage for a political showdown. Unlike the theatrics of Tahir-ul Qadri, a political aspirant who often appears more like an anarchist than a reformer, Khan's call to action carries weight and significance. While Qadri may attract attention, he has failed to make a substantial impact on the power equation, merely dominating media headlines. In contrast, Khan's announcement during his speech in Bahawalpur on 27 June outlined a protest march towards the capital on 14 August, a date marking the independence of the country in 1947 and chosen for its symbolic resonance with the aspirations for change and freedom.

Before embarking on the march, Khan granted a one-month reprieve to the Sharif government, urging them to address the allegations of election rigging. Khan has persistently raised concerns about electoral irregularities, focusing particularly on four constituencies. His demand for a recount is driven by the political and personal necessity of delegitimizing an election that he passionately believed he would win.

However, Khan's call for thumb verification of voters can only materialize if the election tribunals request the National

Database and Registration Authority to undertake the task. As per the current legal framework, the executive cannot interfere with the tribunals' functioning. There is a possibility that Justice Nasirul Mulk, the acting chief election commissioner and future chief justice, may become a target of Khan's political agenda if he intensifies his campaign. Lt Gen. (retd) Abul Qadir Baloch, the minister for states and frontier regions, quickly remarked after Khan's Bahawalpur rally, insinuating that 'the long march is against the judiciary and Election Commission'.

Consequently, the Sharif government anticipates minimal turbulence, with N-League leaders believing that Khan risks pitting his party against the judiciary and may bruise himself in the process.

The battleground of this political struggle remains Punjab, the longstanding stronghold of the Sharif family. Khan's call for political agitation currently finds little resonance in Sindh and Balochistan. Even in Khyber Pakhtunkhwa, reluctance prevails among provincial assembly members to resign en masse.

However, in Punjab, Qadri's return, orchestrated by the Chaudhrys of Gujrat, an influential political family, has compelled Khan to intensify his calls for street agitation. The N-League's fervent pursuit of development projects has invigorated opposition politicians based in Punjab. The provincial government's land acquisition in districts like Faisalabad and Sheikhupura, ostensibly for the establishment of industrial zones operated by Chinese investors, sparked fears among opposition politicians. They worry that completion of these development projects, which boast impressive optics and prove especially enticing to voters during election campaigns, would pose almost insurmountable challenges in the next elections.

Nevertheless, the opposition remains fractured, and the possibility of political alliances appears slim at present. Qadri has already distanced himself from any such alliance, surprising those who believed he would provide foot soldiers for street agitation under a larger political umbrella. Ruling party officials hint at Qadri's U-turns being motivated by veiled threats from the government to investigate his vast assets and scrutinize his tax returns. 'Qadri and the Chaudhrys have been neutralized,' claimed an official from the ruling party.

Khan, on the other hand, remains resolute in his march towards Islamabad, and the government is bracing for renewed political challenges after Ramadan. Unlike Qadri's supporters, who fearlessly confronted the police force, under the hypnotic influence of their leader, it remains to be seen how Pakistan, Tehreek-e-Insaf (PTI)'s cadre, will respond to the potential use of force by state police.

The Sharif family has calculated that the announced protest march, set to hit the capital in mid-August, will prove to be nothing more than a heavy downpour, rather than an extended monsoon.

As the political storm gathers momentum, the nation watched with bated breath, eager to witness the outcome of this clash of ambitions and ideologies.

Chapter 3

A General State of Dysfunction

July 2014

Two episodes grabbed media headlines. Former military spokesperson, Maj. Gen. (retd) Athar Abbas, stunned everyone by criticizing his former boss, Gen. (retd) Pervaiz Kayani, and painting him as the one responsible for aggravating the security condition of the country by dithering over the North Waziristan military offensive. On the civilian side, Interior Minister Chaudhry Nisar Ali Khan remained in the limelight for several days for sulking in a corner, upset over Prime Minister Nawaz Sharif not lending him an ear in key policy decisions. These two issues are, of course, not interlinked but brought to the surface the fissures in the institutional decision-making process and a state of dysfunction within various state organs.

Grumblings over an insular and aloof Prime Minister's Office have been doing the rounds for a while in the capital. Lawmakers complain of having lost access to the prime minister, and only a selected few—with the right genetic and geographical makeup—have the privilege of getting an easy audience with the prime minister.

Pakistan Muslim League Nawaz always had a history of operating through a kitchen cabinet, but this time the kitchen has shrunk to a minuscule level. On 5 July 2014, a Saturday, the interior minister, who was always part of the hallowed kitchen cabinets of the past, finally settled the differences with the premier as both hugged one another in Raiwind Estate. Were these differences over policy matters, as has been speculated? Or were they over egotistical and hierarchical issues, as has been yet more speculation?

Nisar has favoured easing out former military ruler Gen. Pervez Musharraf from the country, but the prime minister has dug in his heels. Nawaz and Nisar also did not agree completely over the outcomes of peace talks with the Taliban. Public differences between officials holding the most important portfolios do not reflect well on the state of governance or its ability to deliver on key, fundamental issues that confront the country. The Nawaz–Nisar bonhomie, exhibited during their meeting, was expected. Nisar peeling away from the ruling party was never a real possibility, at least at that time. Nawaz needs the interior minister to respond to the upcoming challenges posed by both Tahir-ul Qadri and Imran Khan.

Maj. Gen. (retd) Athar Abbas's statement came like a bolt out of the blue. The critique of the former military spokesperson, with a reputation for being a gentle and eloquent officer, portrayed the former army and spy chief as an indecisive and weak military officer. Gen. Kayani, Abbas said, accelerated the slide of Pakistan down the road of instability and insecurity due to his reluctance to take on the militants in North Waziristan. Some have construed the timing of Abbas's statement as intended to bolster the public image of the new army chief, Gen. Raheel Sharif, as a doer and go-getter, compared to a thinking and inscrutable Kayani. Athar Abbas has tried to dismiss any such insinuations and termed the critique an honest answer to a simple question posed by a BBC journalist.

The truth may lie somewhere in the middle. Kayani dexterously maintained the equilibrium of a system he had helped erect after the political turmoil of 2007. His response to a slew of terror attacks on key security installations was dismally lacking. He was compelled by considerations both political and military. But was Kayani's overall security calculus fundamentally different from that of Gen. Sharif? The military is, after all, considered conservative and consistent in its strategic goals and objectives.

Of late, the decision-making process in both civil and military leaderships remains erratic, highly individualized and, quite often, arbitrary. The implications are nightmarish.

* * *

Checkmate?

August 2014

Let's consider scenario number one.

For five years, Nawaz Sharif waited patiently while the PPP completed its tenure at the centre from 2008 to 2013. After initial sniping and botched attempts to undo one another, both political parties decided to live under a policy of 'reconciliation' and joined hands whenever there was a threat from the powerful establishment. Nawaz Sharif's political party, PML–N, was always the party in waiting, and the sudden rise of Imran Khan after October 2011 forced it to pace up on signature mega projects. But it never really saw Khan as a real contender for the seat of power in Islamabad. In the May 2013 elections, the business and industry sectors, battered by power outages, saw more benefit in siding with Nawaz than with an inexperienced Khan. The public, by and large, felt the same and handed Nawaz Sharif a comfortable majority in parliament. Nawaz conquered the country again, despite being thrown out by the military after the 1999 coup.

Now back in power, Nawaz Sharif feels invincible. Years of exile have shaped and altered him—he has come of age. Nawaz

Sharif now has bigger ambitions and clarity of purpose. The notion of civilian supremacy is even more ingrained in his mind. The thumping electoral win is a validation. The military, always the overbearing and overarching presence, must focus on what a military must focus on. The Musharraf years sank the public perception of the military, even as Kayani puts it back on the mend, it will always be hamstrung and unable to orchestrate another coup. Nawaz Sharif and his inner clique banked on this calculation. On the east lies India, with immense possibilities for business and profit. Nawaz Sharif thinks like an entrepreneur. Kashmir was already left on the cold burner under Musharraf and can be sidestepped with ease. The military will grumble, but not boil over. Afghanistan is a cause of instability and needs addressing. Nawaz Sharif feels there should be a rapprochement on both of these borders. And within these borders, Musharraf needs to be punished.

So, Nawaz Sharif forges ahead. Meanwhile, his inner circle is becoming increasingly dismissive towards others—both civilian politicians and military generals. The civilian opposition has been neutralized, but the military establishment retains its core power and the ability to exercise it. There is resentment and anger within the ranks. The institution cannot be maligned, they stress. The central objectives of the institution and the state are at odds with the narrative that Nawaz is constructing. They helped Nawaz Sharif get the majority on the night of the elections when Imran's tide seemed to be in full swing. The Deep State was at work that evening. It is now time to pull the plug. Imran is asked to rally his hypnotized youth. The experience of the 2009 Long March provides the blueprint: more people, more power. But Imran bungles up. He cannot manage or handle the details. His rhetoric does not affect other political parties, and the necessary numbers don't add up. The promise of 14 August fizzles away. But Khan cannot be left bleeding. After he loses hope and goes back to sleep in Bani Gala, his palatial residence on the top of the Islamabad hills, he receives an expression of support and the logistics of that support. So, Imran picks himself up. Tahir-ul Qadri is asked to bolster Imran. In synchronized words and steps, both populist leaders breach the Red Zone and camp outside the parliament, threatening to breach even further. Inside, troops of the mythic 111 brigade, which looks after the security of the General Headquarters (GHQ) in Rawalpindi and often provides security to important buildings in the capital, are already stationed.

Nawaz is checkmated. It is just a matter of time.

Consider the second scenario.

Khan has achieved whatever he has aspired to and aimed for. No one thought he could make it to the national team. He made it and won the 1992 World Cup. Nobody thought he could build the country's first cancer hospital. He did it. Nobody thought he would survive in politics; he would always writhe on the sidelines. He emerged as a political force in the 2013 elections. In the run-up to the vote, he saw people vying for change. He saw a revulsion toward the status quo. People— the poor and the rich, the provincial and the urbane—saw him as the agent for change. He was to be the next prime minister. Khan has always been the man with the most deeply ingrained sense of self. The forces of the status quo are wronging the winner. And these wrongs cannot be addressed in the system that the status quo perpetuates. He decides to once again do what no one else thought he could. But people did not join him in the droves he expected. There is stagnation and inertia, and he needs to push harder. He will not bend, and he will not compromise. People will come around, just like they did in the past two decades. He has already sensed a weakness in the Nawaz Sharif camp and will keep holding Nawaz Sharif's neck until it snaps.

Tahir-ul Qadri, the religious preacher with the ambitions of a politician, also feels wronged. In his own eyes, he was always the talented one, the educated one and the blessed one. He wants to spread these blessings. He hates the Sharifs because they shun him as a mere preacher. He is much more than that. He is a visionary. He is a messiah (in his own eyes). Since leaving Pakistan, he has built a network around the world. It is financially stable, and it is theologically and intellectually sounder than the corrupt politicians and their corrupt system. Nobody can be a bigger Lenin or Marx, Qadri himself says. Since 2013, when the police in Lahore shot and killed several of his supporters, Qadri has learned a valuable lesson. This time, he will not back down. So, what if Imran has launched his struggle side by side? Both can stay together and strengthen themselves until Nawaz falls. Then they will fight it out amongst themselves. Qadri feels his cadre is more resilient and tenacious. Imran's cadre will sing, dance and tire itself. The army will have to stand alongside the power of the people.

Nawaz is checkmated. It is just a matter of time.

But consider this: this is not a simple game of chess. It is a variant. It is a game of Kriegsspiel (where two players play the game, unaware of the move of the other's piece—and in the presence of a referee). And whenever one of the players makes an illegal move, the referee will come to the fore and say: 'impossible.'

* * *

What will happen on 30 November?

The daggers are drawn, but will they make the final cut?

November 2014

Islamabad is being barricaded again. The shipping containers have sprouted ubiquitously from the roads and sidewalks. Khan is once again promising a revolution like never before.

The government is pretending to be sitting pretty, having managed to cling on despite appearing to be teetering perilously close to an ouster a few months ago. Khan seems further emboldened and does not show any signs of letting up. It's simply not the nature of man. Both sides feel that the duel fought out on Constitution Avenue battered and bruised the other side more.

Expectations this time, therefore, are higher. The sense of confidence needed to win the second round has swelled. Khan's party has learned from its past failings and has campaigned more vigorously to bring out more and more people on the streets this time around. The government has already disarmed its police force, handing them batons and withdrawing guns and bullets. There can be a tidal wave of people, but without violence, it would not rock their boat.

It's déjà vu—30 November is already feeling like 14 August.

There have been, however, some fundamental shifts in the political landscape. There was an abiding sense that some elements of the military intelligence establishment were supporting the protesters. But a consensus was lacking, and since the man who really calls the shots, the chief, did not throw his weight behind the opposition, the movement fizzled out. There has been ample anecdotal evidence to support such speculations, but, as always, there is no smoking gun. Taking the conspiracy theory at face value, one is compelled to infer that for now, with the change of guard at Aabpara, as the ISI headquarters is sometimes referred to, there will inevitably be a review of strategy. The dynamics of mid-August will simply not work in the last leg of the year. If there must be some puppeteering, it will now come at another time, in another context and in another shape and form.

The biggest point of discord between the military and Prime Minister Nawaz Sharif in the early days was relations with India. Trade and normalization of relations were high on the premier's agenda. Now, it's on the back burner. There is no sense of immediacy. The back-pedalling has been obvious, and in recent weeks, Kashmir, the perennial issue between the countries, is back in the limelight. The aggressive posture of the Indians has muted the doves in the government, and the hawks have made a resurgence. On national security and policy matters, the political government is singing the same tune as the military establishment.

During the tumult of the protests in August, Tahir-ul Qadri's followers posed the most formidable challenge to the government's writ and authority. After the sudden retreat, Qadri has not yet announced any plans to mount yet another offensive on the capital. Instead, he is busy consolidating himself in other regions where his support among the locals is high. Government officials take a more sanguine view of Qadri's about-face and say that he has been 'neutralized'.

Another big factor that added to the sense of vulnerability of the government was former ruler Gen. Pervez Musharraf's treason trial. With the latest special court directive throwing the net around the alleged abettors of the November 2007 emergency rule, the trial proceedings have become even more complicated and, most certainly, even more protracted. If there is no immediate sense of conviction against the former army chief, the discontent within the military ranks against the perceived humiliation of their former boss will remain under the surface and seem less threatening and intimidating to the government.

So, while the most potent threats have diminished, what greater damage can Khan do on 30 November when he plans to launch yet another street protest? Apparently not a lot, if the damage must be assessed in terms of the potential of forcing the ruling government out. On the other side, Khan has achieved substantially in terms of entrenching himself as the real opposition and challenger to the established political parties. He can further steel himself if his party works out with the government—and other political parties—an effective and transparent overhaul of the tainted and dysfunctional electoral system. That would ensure that whenever the next elections take place, his party's prominence and further rise would be inevitable.

On 30 November, Khan and Prime Minister Nawaz Sharif will not be gladiators in a ring. The joust between the two is more like one side aiming at the political death of the other through a thousand cuts. Insisting that 30 November would be a cataclysmic day that would rock the foundations of the government is a bit of a stretch. It would nevertheless be a day of high drama and TV-friendly fracas. After all, the show must go on.

Chapter 4

Government Running Out of Fuel and Ideas

January 2015

It is astounding how easily a political government gets upended. Politicians, who have ruled for decades, appear as clueless as a layperson when it comes to dealing with the issues of governance and economy. Even a faint whiff of street agitation gets the rulers scrambling for cover. Panic sets in in their straw houses with the appearance of the slightest frown from the military.

Hamstrung and dysfunctional, political governments in Pakistan lurch along in a grim mockery of democratic rule. Worse is the failure and lack of will to improve, to get out of the morass, and to be able to do something. Hollow-sounding slogans are constantly fed to the masses. Cheap gimmickry is employed to throw dirt in the eyes of the people. Platitudes of the worst type are used repeatedly. For a country yearning for democracy, its form of democracy degenerates into a revolting display of crass nepotism and crude opportunism.

For Prime Minister Nawaz Sharif, the failings of his government should be an immense cause of discomfort and embarrassment. The scion of an industrial and business empire, the prime minister seems unable to hold back the slide of his government deeper and deeper into failure and incompetence.

From the tragic sights of police opening fire on political opponents to the current displays of public desperation at petrol filling stations, the government cuts a sorry figure, disconnected from reality, and mired in controversies and a continuous series of missteps.

Nothing really explains the perverse performance. What was sold as the winning ticket of the PML–N before the elections seems to be its biggest predicament. The ministers appear washed-up and bumbling, odd and tragic caricatures of their pre-election pretence and rhetoric. The edifice of the PML–N election manifesto seems to be in a shambles.

Almost half of last year was lost in a gruelling battle with Imran Khan and Tahir-ul Qadri. Imran harangued the public for several months, mostly in desperate and struggling situations. Having lost the plot soon after initiating his protest campaign, Imran drained himself and his supporters. Now, he has vowed to transform Khyber Pakhtunkhwa Province into the imaginary wonderland that he was selling to the youth. But he, too, now suffers from a dent in credibility and authenticity. And the less said about Tahir-ul Qadri, the better. His 'Green Revolution', propelled by the alleged millions of supporters, also turned into a pipe dream as the protest sit-in was wrapped up suddenly in utter ignominy.

The Sharif government should have capitalized on the failings of its most bitter and formidable political opponents by seizing the political initiative. But the government seems to have run out of fuel, both literally and metaphorically.

In a rapidly changing political environment, its ministers appear complacent and quiescent. Shirking responsibility, each minister passed the buck with an inexcusable smile. It also said something of the chutzpah of the second-most powerful man in the federal cabinet, Finance Minister Ishaq Dar, when he came up with the most improbable defence about a conspiracy hatched against the government.

Prime Minister Nawaz Sharif expressed his 'extreme displeasure', but not the ire that was needed. The ire and anger should have been visible if he wanted to salvage his image and government.

The Nawaz League powerhouse is built around 'political relatives' who act as scaffolding for the big Sharif. Each of these controls a certain faction that is perilously holding together the big Sharif. They cannot get fired or reshuffled because it would imbalance the shaky structure and bring everything down altogether.

Asif Ali Zardari's government was no less a disaster in many ways, but Zardari was smarter in letting off steam. He changed and shuffled his ministers and sacrificed a prime minister even though he risked the appearance of weakness but displayed flexibility and elasticity.

In the House of Sharifs, political expediency and family loyalty reign supreme over the need for fair process and transparent accountability. It is a terrible miscalculation, in contravention of the needs of the time. But it also shines a torch on the kind of politics and politicians here.

Chapter 5

Status Quo

November 2015

Last year, around this time, the Nawaz government was on tenterhooks. Imran Khan's sit-in was going nowhere, but it was not letting the government move anywhere either. The military, ever the final arbiter, saw the pendulum swing in its favour—the army chief was on the ascendant—and many had wished for it to redraw the political equation. Fast forward, and there has been quite a reversal. Nawaz Sharif has managed to survive—despite what some analysts have described as a pyrrhic escape—the political challenge.

Khan has faced some setbacks, partly due to domestic troubles and partly because of political miscalculations. The momentum of his party, PTI, has been lost; its juggernaut has come to a grinding halt. Imran now concedes that elections will take place on time, in 2018, and that he will divert his attention to improving Khyber Pakhtunkhwa.

From being the biggest threat that could send the government packing because of street protests, Imran and his party have been reduced to the usual troublemakers. However, Khan has a new trick up his sleeve. The Khyber Pakhtunkhwa (KPK) provincial government now intends to start opposing the China–Pakistan Economic Corridor (CEPC), the mega project

21

with the Chinese, even going to the extent of threatening to stop land acquisition in the province. However, such a course of action risks a confrontation not only with the Sharif government but also with the military, which is equally invested in Chinese projects in the country.

For Nawaz Sharif, the biggest challenge remains the government itself. After taking a breather from the pounding of the political opposition, he must ensure performance and improve governance. Within the ruling party, the internal fissures remain evident but not wide enough to cause a deadlock. The local body polls have only reinforced the earlier political permutations, and no major upsets are expected.

The changed political environment has added to the confidence of the prime minister. Increasingly confident and exuding a self-assured air, Nawaz has changed his tack. The jaunts to various parts of the country have multiplied, and the government's media managers are keen to portray the premier as being as agile and quick in action as was the hallmark of Army Chief Gen. Raheel Sharif.

In the battle of optics, both civilians and the military are competing with equal alacrity. It is also a measure of the prevalent civil–military divide.

Government ministers have repeated ad nauseam that they are on the same page with the military, but it is clearly an eyewash. The military has not bothered to issue similar statements. Instead, it keeps on exhorting the government to improve governance and take political ownership of the effort against militancy. With differences persisting over the fundamentals, both sides remain unable to move forward or step back from their entrenched positions.

The army chief, Gen. Raheel Sharif, has had his high time in terms of media exposure and now seems to be on a diminishing curve. Overexposure in the media has now started to seep in.

Gen. Sharif's visit to the United States lacked glittery media headlines and was short on deliverables. While meeting with the US vice president was dubbed the 'crowning moment', the foreign sojourns have achieved another feat: being the first Asian to be awarded Brazil's Order of Merit award.

But perhaps it is an unremarkable accolade that the military's media machine has taken pride in. In essence, the award means little and perhaps shows how the preoccupations within the corridors of power have shifted.

This time, the advent of winter has come with a cooling of political temperatures as well. For the rambunctious television news networks, which thrive on controversy and sensationalism, it can be a terribly boring time.

Chapter 6

Recapping the Ides of March

April 2016

Caesar, the Roman emperor, was famously warned by a soothsayer about the 'ides of March', a phrase immortalized by Shakespeare. It might be instructive to reflect on what happened in March in the 'land of the pure'.

Sometime in early March, Pakistani authorities arrested an Indian naval officer in Balochistan. The arrest is portrayed as a coup in the world of spies and clandestine networks. The Indian intelligence agent ran a vast network and was responsible for mayhem and chaos in Balochistan and Karachi, officials say.

On 25 March, Pakistan summons the Indian High Commissioner to the foreign ministry, lodges a strong protest and hands out a demarche. On 27 March, a suicide bomber rips through Gulshan-e-Iqbal Park in Lahore, one of the largest public parks in the city. Ordinarily the park attracts many visitors, but that Sunday, the crowd was larger than usual, including dozens of Christian families celebrating Easter. At least seventy people were killed in one of the worst attacks in Lahore in recent years.

Jamaat-e-Ahrar, which claimed responsibility for the Lahore bombing, had also claimed responsibility for a bomb that tore through a bus carrying government employees in

Peshawar earlier in the month. Operation Zarb-e-Azb is nearing completion in the province, with the last redoubts of militants eradicated in the tribal regions, officials say.

The slow-burning blowback has continued, first in the form of the Army Public School massacre and later in attacks on a university and court complex in Charsadda, Khyber Pakhtunkhwa province. Jamaat-e-Ahrar, however, warns the political rulers of Punjab province that the bombing was to show that now their aim is directed at the Sharif brothers.

Prime Minister Sharif holds meetings with his senior officials and vows to avenge the innocent deaths. He also addresses the nation, a rare move in his style of governance and leadership.

Simultaneously, the army chief, Gen. Raheel Sharif, also holds meetings with his commanders and orders intelligence-based operations in Punjab, the political fortress of the Sharifs. The announcement comes through a series of posts by the military on Twitter, the social networking service.

The younger brother, Shehbaz Sharif, and his acolytes in the provinces have persistently claimed that there is no need for a military operation; the police and other civilian security apparatus are enough to counter the militants. The provincial police chief claims that there is no 'safe haven for terrorists', no 'no-go area', even in the southern parts, where militancy is supposed to be thriving.

Soon thousands of people are rounded up, described mostly as 'facilitators,' but it remains unclear what connection they had with the Lahore bombing. Within two days, 95 per cent of those detained were released. It also remains unclear why no move was made against them earlier if they posed such a grave threat. The provincial apex meeting does not hold any new meetings post-bombing, but it remains unclear why it could not authorize an operation against militants and their facilitators earlier.

While the bombing rattled Lahore, thousands of religious zealots, condemning the execution of Mumtaz Qadri, had also gathered in Rawalpindi. The occasion was 'Chehlum' of Qadri, a ritual observed the day after forty days of the death of a person. But the supporters were in a hurry—and an even more of a hurry to reach Islamabad. While the Islamabad and Rawalpindi administrations watch on, the protesters move into the capital, easily removing occasional hurdles, and ensconce themselves at D-Chowk, which provides a clear view of the parliament.

Democracy is again in peril; the civilians are slow in responding to the challenges, while the military wants more support from the people.

Suddenly, there is a loud cacophony about how weak Nawaz Sharif has been on militancy and how reluctant the PML–N has been to move against militancy in Punjab. Accusations against Nawaz for being soft on India are spreading on social media. Some come up with alleged evidence that a few technical experts employed by a sugar mill owned by the Sharifs were Indians, blaming them as Research and Analysis Wing (RAW) agents. Some even go to the extent of declaring the thrice elected prime minister, who holds a majority in the parliament, as a 'security risk'.

It is also in the same month that, down in the southern part of the country, former president and army chief Pervez Musharraf manages to fly out to Dubai, effectively evading treason proceedings against him.

During the ten years of his rule, the Muttahida Qaumi Movement (MQM) was his staunch supporter inside the parliament and on the streets of Karachi. The then mayor of Karachi, Mustafa Kamal, was hugged and kissed by an overwhelmed Altaf Hussain, grateful for the work the young man had done for the city. But now, MQM is in the dock, accused of taking funding and directions from RAW. There is no effort to ask Musharraf about the MQM of his days and its links with the hostile intelligence agency, let alone any effort to hold him accountable.

While Musharraf suddenly finds his health recuperated enough to hold a political meeting in Dubai, Mustafa Kamal leads a cleansing mission in the port city. Mustafa Kamal was unaware of the sinister underpinnings of his political party for decades and has suddenly found the courage and conviction to shed away his past and fly the national flag with the enthusiasm and passion of a convert.

Meanwhile, the Iranian president visits Pakistan, ostensibly to improve and enhance economic ties. But the visit is overshadowed by the controversy about whether Gen. Raheel asked the Iranians to be tough on Indian intelligence operatives on their soil or not. The Iranian president denies such talk, but the military claims—through tweets on social media—that such concerns were, in fact, raised.

Privately, Iranians were upset that sensitive matters of diplomacy were discussed publicly. The Pakistani foreign office, which could take up the concerns in appropriate diplomatic language, remains mum during this episode. An investigative journalist raised questions about the 'tweet policy' in an opinion article in a leading English newspaper, expressing concern that it is negatively impacting civil–military relations. But there was a strong rebuff by the military spokesperson, who said that the opinion piece was an 'attempt to question the performance of the Army'.

The parallel, competing decisions taken by civilians and the military were vividly apparent in March. The differences to counter the challenges they mutually face portend a greater crisis in the making.

Chapter 7

The Politics of Vanity

August 2016

The problem when you become Imran Khan is that you just cannot stay Imran Khan. You want to be even bigger . . . bigger than anything and everything.

On Monday, Khan tweeted a picture of himself, drenched with sweat, standing proudly with his two sons by his sides. Sunlight filtered through a sky laden with heavy clouds in the background. It was a proud moment: the Khans had conquered Miranjani, the highest peak in Galliat, the hill tracts between Abottabad and Murree. Next up was to 'conquer' the mountain of corruption from 7 August, the great athlete-turned-politician tweeted.

It was yet again another bombastic and sanctimonious announcement, so typical of the style of politics of Khan. If, at sixty-three, he can conquer the highest peak in Galliat with the agility of his teenage sons, his cultish followers will argue that nothing can stop him from conquering the mountains of corruption. After all, the slogan against corruption has been the bedrock of his political message for most of his political career. The Panama Leaks gave him a new lease on life after the earlier mantra of rigging failed to jolt most of the population from its apathy. But Imran Khan, being Imran Khan, does not give up. It is a fact he reiterates in every interview. 'You cannot lose if you don't accept defeat' has been a sentence repeated ad nauseam.

Now, rejuvenated after the holiday up north with his boys, Khan is gearing up to start yet another agitation campaign. This time, it is a 'protest campaign'. No more tsunamis. No more 'dharna' (sit in). It is just a plain and simple protest campaign.

It is always telling to watch Khan's interviews before he embarks on his mission to jolt the masses out of their slumber. The talking points are the same; he will never deviate from the scripted words and arguments in the interviews and during the rallies. There is a massive repetition overdose. As outlined in his most recent TV appearances, here is what we know about Imran's plans: the conquerors will start from Peshawar and drive down to Islamabad before finally reaching Imran Khan's real political destination, Lahore.

All along the way, Imran will address rallies bursting with humidity and infused with the spirit of change and revolution. There will be delirious dancing. There will be boisterous songs. There will be feverish live coverage every time Imran Khan holds the lectern. And, each time, he will narrate his cricketing laurels, and each time the crowd will cheer. Evening talk shows will pore over the speeches, and the prophets of doom will make their predictions of the end of time. It will not really matter that after the thumping defeat in the Kashmir elections, Imran had vowed to speed up work to show how his team can transform the province. Such vows will drown out the loud noise of those wishing desperately for revolution.

A revolution on the streets, a revolution through agitation, a revolution through such mass hysteria that its proponents hope the military is forced to take over. There is no need for a democratic process or parliamentary debate. Who really wants to bore oneself to death with dull parliamentary committees and proceedings of the house? Legislation can wait.

But worn-out speeches, high on rhetoric and low on substance, cannot wait.

Meanwhile, the cultish followers will make YouTube and Snapchat videos of a glamorous and swashbuckling crusader. There will be Facebook posts and there will be Twitter trends.

And all this while, Khan will continue to tell the people how it is the defining moment, how it is the last chance, and how we are standing on the last edge of the precipice. But it will be just another huge physical exercise, draining bodies and exhausting minds.

But Khan loves it. He himself says he cannot sit idle. After 2014, Khan started getting bored while sitting at home. He wanted to hit the road and it is no different this time. What is the real purpose and objective of this 'campaign' when similar campaigns in the past have not resonated with the voters? Khan does not really provide an answer to this. Voters are dismissed as lacking dignity and willing slaves of the Sharif Empire.

After the shaking and shoving of a few weeks, the PTI conquerors will recede, and Imran Khan will go back to the UK for a few days, as he mostly does. Meanwhile, the cultish followers will keep grieving that the nation does not deserve an honest man like their leader. It is the same old song and dance. There will be yet another reprise.

And for those who want to know how and why Nawaz Sharif is erring, one does not really have to spell it out here. 7 August is not far away. Imran Khan is coming to conquer the airwaves and tell that story.

Chapter 8

Political Theatre

October 2016

Politics is part theatre. It is about capturing the imagination of the electorate. This month Sheikh Rashid played this part to perfection. While police barricaded all roads leading to the Lal Haveli, the political base of the wily politician from Rawalpindi, Sheikh Rashid used social media to tease the authorities and entertain his supporters. Sheikh Rashid knows his limitations. He does not have many supporters in his constituency and owes his National Assembly seat to PTI's support in the 2013 General Elections. He has his hand on the pulse of popular public sentiment, and expresses these sentiments in the wittiest political phrases.

The image of a portly Sheikh Rashid running, flanked by four supporters, will remain etched in the public's imagination for a long time. Equally entertaining was his climbing a DSNG van and lighting up a cigar. Videos featuring him sitting on the back of a motorcycle and riding through the maze of narrow streets in the inner parts of the city went viral.

It does not really matter that there was no actual police chase. The videos did not show police officers scrambling after the portly politician, dressed like a shady character from the movies. There were no blaring police sirens in the background.

But Sheikh Rashid was seen as a man on the run, evading arrest in a breathless manner. It was a perfect political theatre. 'Catch me if you can,' Sheikh Rashid tweeted.

On the other hand, Khan failed to keep his promise to reach Lal Haveli. All day long, he kept sitting inside his grand villa, most of the time donning his stylish sunglasses. While many supporters waited for him at the gate of his residence, Imran kept dithering. Understandably, it was almost impossible to breach the security cordon thrown around by the government without risking arrest. But Khan should have at least tried to be seen as trying to break the security ring.

The image of a politician scuffling with ham-handed security officials always plays to the politician's and his supporters' advantage. It would have made perfect television. But Imran let the opportunity slip. Instead, later in the evening, he comfortably appeared outside of his residence, wearing a leather jacket, and offered the most improbable defence for what can be construed as a lack of courage: he was preserving his energies for the 2 November showdown. PTI often fails to capitalize on political theatre, unlike its ally—the wily Sheikh Rashid. Anti-Climax has defined most of the agitation campaigns and efforts by PTI. It remains to be seen whether 2 November will be any different.

Meanwhile, Prime Minister Nawaz Sharif extended his sacrificial offering to the military. The sacking of Pervez Rashid, the information minister, should come as no surprise. Non-elected members are the most expendable. The press statement by the Prime Minister's Office is telling, though. It acknowledges that *Dawn*'s 6 November story was 'planted'.

The statement also alleges 'a lapse on the part of' the former information minister. The news was announced to the media in the evening. Earlier, Prime Minister Nawaz Sharif addressed a rally in a town near Lahore. He appeared confident and defiant in the face of the challenges that stared him in the face. Prime Minister Nawaz Sharif assured his supporters that his government would complete its term. Such assertions can be taken with scepticism. Back in the 1990s, Prime Minister Nawaz Sharif threw in the towel soon after announcing that he would not take dictation.

The coming weeks will tell how different it is this time around. In politics, timing is everything. Prime Minister Sharif chose to sacrifice his trusted ally just days before the 2 November capital lockdown plan by PTI. The former information minister's head was offered to placate the military, and he might not be the real mastermind of the leak. Prime Minister Nawaz Sharif is also keeping other cards close to his chest. The announcement of the new army chief is being kept a closely guarded secret.

Will it be enough to avert the political crisis and the impending showdown?

* * *

Inviting the 'third force'

24 October 2016

Khan has seemingly thrown away all pretence of being a political leader who has any regard for democratic processes or parliamentary institutions. In his latest press conference, Imran Khan acted with supreme nonchalance about the possibility of a military takeover due to his plan to lay siege to the capital next month. In his usual style, Khan said that the responsibility for the toppling of the democratic setup would rest with Prime Minister Nawaz Sharif. The ease with which Khan absolves himself of any responsibility is breathtaking and appalling. It gives credence to an increasing public perception that Khan's politics—or attempt at politics—has become singularly obsessed with ousting the prime minister. Institution building, strengthening the democratic process and working within the constitutional framework are the least of his priorities.

No one can deny that the Sharif family must be held accountable for their alleged corruption. The revelations in the Panama Papers must be probed. But it certainly does not mean that all the institutional and constitutional frameworks of the country must be sidestepped because they do not suit the political ambitions of Khan. For the leader of PTI, all institutions, sans the military, are beholden to the prime minister. It casts a dark shadow over the judiciary, which has tried so hard to appear independent since the 2007 lawyers' movement.

While delegitimizing everything except the military, Khan appears as a fifth columnist for non-democratic forces. Khan seems the least concerned about this image. He keeps giving examples of how Western democracies work, and how hundreds of thousands of people take to the streets when in disagreement with their governments. But he very conveniently omits to answer whether the 2003 anti-war protesters in London laid siege to the city and paralyzed it for weeks and months. Ever since the 2014 sit-in, Khan talks about his days and nights spent inside the shipping container with a deep sense of romanticism and nostalgia. It makes one wonder whether Khan sees himself as a political leader or the commander of a medieval army that is about to run through the defences of an enemy army's fortress.

In pursuing his obsession to become the prime minister, Khan has led a wide section of society towards a dead end, where they are oblivious to the ramifications of their incendiary rhetoric and exclusionary tactics. Consequently, polarization within society is becoming acuter, and the seeds of fascism have been sown in the youth and the middle-class. And only the leader of PTI will be elated when they bloom into wild cactuses. Already, the political body of the country has become so poisonous that the ruling party is accused of being hand-in-glove with the enemy country, that is, India. Such labelling of the political class as the enemy's agents is not new, but there are bound to be long-term consequences when gradually all civilians are dubbed and maligned as anti-state and agents of hostile international forces.

As the country heads towards the 'apocalyptic' 2 November 'Islamabad lockdown' in PTI's terms, the civil–military imbalance also hangs in sharp contrast. While the prime minister is intent on having his last word on the army chief's successor, some analysts have commented that the military has forbidden the civilian government from making any announcements before the first week of November. Such calls, if true, are indeed unfortunate and certainly unconstitutional.

Civilians must be held accountable for their wrongdoing and transgressions against the law, but to invite the 'third power', even if inadvertently, is a course that must be condemned. Imran Khan should not plough the land for non-democratic forces or even his dictatorial instincts.

Chapter 9

Dawn Leaks: The Who's Who

October 2016

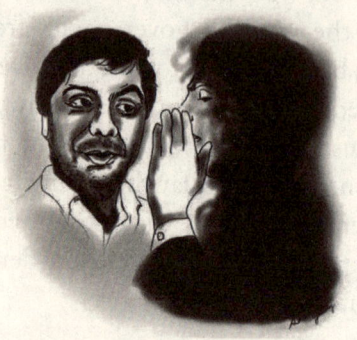

Dawn Assistant Editor Cyril Almeida was tipped off by anonymous sources regarding sensitive details of a national security meeting between the government and the military officials held at the Prime Minister's House on 3 October 2016. The news article resulted in a big political crisis as the military accused the Sharif government of leaking sensitive state information.

On 7 October 2016, Almeida wrote in *Dawn* about the increasing tension between the civilian and military leadership over how the country deals with Islamist terrorists.

'In a blunt, orchestrated and unprecedented warning, the civilian government has informed the military leadership of a growing international isolation of Pakistan and sought consensus on several key actions by the state,' Almeida wrote, citing different sources. 'The message: military-led intelligence agencies are not to interfere if law enforcement acts against militant groups that are banned or until now considered off-limits for civilian action,' Almeida wrote in the front-page news article.

The federal government, which is allegedly behind the leak, is promising to hold an inquiry to trace the source whose conversation with *Dawn* staffer, Cyril Almeida, has caused tremors in the country's civil-military landscape.

Official sources say all four provincial chief ministers along with the chief minister of Gilgit-Baltistan were part of the 3 October meeting, which was held at the Prime Minister's House.

The following cabinet ministers and high-ranking officials were in attendance: 1. Muhammad Ishaq Dar, minister for finance; 2. Chaudhry Nisar Ali Khan, minister for interior; 3. Pervaiz Rashid, minister for information; 4. Gen. Raheel Sharif, chief of army staff; 5. Tariq Fatemi, Special Assistant to the Prime Minister (SAPM); 6. Lt Gen. (retd) Nasser Khan Janjua, National Security Adviser (NSA); 7. Lt. Gen. Rizwan Akhtar, director-general ISI; 8. Aizaz Ahmad Ch, foreign secretary 9. Aftab Sultan, director-general IB; 10. Fawad Hasan Fawad, SPM; 11. Maj. Gen. Sahir Shamshad Mirza, director-general MO and 12. Maj Gen Nadeem Zaki Manj, director-general Military Intelligence.

The military officials are ostensibly not believed to be behind the leak. The speculation windmill has churned out the following government names—some not in attendance—to be behind the 'leak':

Khawaja Muhammad Asif

Asif has been a vociferous critic of the military's overarching role in the civilian body politic. In return, the military has only begrudgingly accepted him as the defence minister—and he gets short shrift during military ceremonies. His critics have often used a video of Asif making an impassioned speech in the parliament during the early 2000s to portray him as 'anti-army'. Asif, many argue, would have relished a spectacle of the military eating some humble pie.

Mohiuddin Wani

Wani has tireless energy and a sharp mind that indulges and influences the media, especially electronic media. Of late, however, he has stopped attending security briefings. Some say his absence offers perfect plausible deniability, but Wani vehemently denied his involvement in this episode. The interior minister in his 13 October briefing said that those suspected of leaking the story will not be allowed to go abroad. Wani was already out of the country by that time, part of the entourage of the prime minister to Azerbaijan.

Pervaiz Rashid

Soft-spoken and mild-mannered yet known for his acerbic and sarcastic comments towards the military establishment, it is common knowledge that Rashid has found it hard to forget the suffering endured after the 1999 military coup. As the head honcho of the government's information ministry, some inevitably speculate that he could be the source through which the news travelled.

Aizaz Chaudhry

The foreign secretary is known to be a cautious and calculated diplomat. *Dawn*'s story mentioned the foreign secretary apprising the civilian leadership about China's growing impatience with Pakistan's policy towards leaders of certain banned militant groups. However, sources tell *Nation* that Chinese concerns reached the GHQ last year and were not new information in the 3 October meeting.

Tariq Fatemi

A diplomat, known more for his turf war with Sartaj Aziz, Fatemi's name has also circulated as the leaker. Apart from his battle to control the foreign office bureaucracy, Fatemi has been busy doing the impossible job of convincing Western diplomats about the country's policies.

Musadik Malik

Glib and loquacious, Musadik is also included in the chatter as there are guesses he could have engineered the move. Some in the capital speculate that the Wani–Musadik duo could have orchestrated the leak with the blessing of the infamous PM House media cell.

Aftab Sultan

The head of the Intelligence Bureau (IB) is a trusted ally of the prime minister. In the past, IB has been known to embark on plans and strategies to minimize the influence of the military's intelligence agencies.

Fawad Hasan Fawad

Fawad's name has been bandied about. He derives a lot of power due to his proximity with the prime minister and some have suspected him to be the source. Others believe that Fawad is too mired in his bureaucratic playing field and not capable of launching sophisticated media campaigns.

Outlook

It is difficult to believe that the government will seriously pursue finding the source since the alleged person is believed to be amongst its own ranks. *Dawn* Assistant Editor Cyril Almeida has already been struck off the Exit Control List and any subsequent inquiry into the matter is expected to fizzle out.

Most analysts agree that the leak was intended to gain a tactical advantage for the civilians at a time when the appointment of the new army chief was just weeks away.

The military's top corps commanders issued a press statement, expressing concern over the 'feeding of [a] false and fabricated story of an important security meeting' held at Prime Minster House. The corps commanders also viewed it as a 'breach of national security'.

It portends that the military will not leave the government off the hook that easily.

Chapter 10

The Message

What made Imran Khan change his mind?

November 2016

On the morning of 1 November, Khan, wearing a bright red T-shirt, appeared before the television cameras and said he would emerge out of his residence to lead one million followers the next day. The showdown was to be played out in the streets of Islamabad. 'Let's see who can stop me,' he challenged.

Earlier in the night, hundreds of PTI supporters from Khyber Pakhtunkhwa clashed with police in a hail of rubber bullets and clouds of tear gas. Despite the charges, the security ring proved difficult to breach. Pervez Khattak was nonetheless determined. His men kept pushing forward. The cranes removed containers, and vehicles managed to pass through. But the advance was again blocked at the Burhan interchange.

Khan was watching the battle on television, surrounded by his close aides. Down at the foothill, the protesters in the temporary encampments also observed the effort of Khyber Pakhtunkhwa reinforcement. They were all filled with hope and anticipation. But the signs were not hopeful. The government's plan of multiple security rings and free use of force exhausted the PTI flanks. Finally, Khan picked up the phone. Turn back, the captain said to his player.

Meanwhile, the government was also tentative. It knew it had been able to dent the opponent's momentum. But the prospect of a violent clash still loomed. The screaming international headlines of violence and deaths would ruin its already battered image. A government that had tried—through 'Dawn Leaks'—to burnish its democratic credentials and its commitment to civilian supremacy could not afford to be drawn into a vortex of deadly political violence. It sent some signals to the opponent. The intermediaries said they received mixed signals.

By midday on 1 November, Sheikh Rashid Ahmed had met Khan. The wily politician felt resentful and let down. He complained that Khan should have joined him last week at the Lal Haveli rally. But Khan talked him down. 'How can I lead the millions of people on 2 November if I get arrested?' he said.

Khan's confidence, however, belied the reality on the ground. Despondency had already started to descend over Bani Gala. The numbers were terribly small. The people from Islamabad and nearby Rawalpindi did not join the call for protest. While some action kept happening outside Khan's residence, the rest of the city remained peaceful, almost indifferent, and unconcerned. The people of the capital had shrugged off the latest protest call.

Moreover, most of Punjab looked the other way. Days of a police crackdown and the arrest of hundreds of workers emasculated the party's mobilizing base. Mid-level party workers were on the run. Some were trying to reach Islamabad while evading the police. Others were hiding in their towns and cities with friends or friends of friends.

Most of the Punjab leadership was already in Islamabad; the main leaders were at the chairman's home, the headquarters of the latest putsch. And the rest of the province, reluctantly, kept sitting on the fence. 'We felt very frustrated. Punjab was not mobilized properly,' said a party official. 'Everyone knew it, but no one was talking about it.'

By midday Tuesday, it was evident to the PTI leadership that the Khyber Pakhtunkhwa reinforcements would not be able to make it to Islamabad. Already, morale was low in and outside the Bani Gala. When a convoy from Lahore, led by Andaleeb Abbas, reached there, it had only forty participants. And when they tried to force their way through the police barrier on Korang Road, the police greeted them with brute force. Abbas was briefly detained, along with a few others.

'For the top leadership sitting on the top of the hill, it was the final indicator,' the party official said. 'They realised that there wouldn't be enough people tomorrow. It already looked over.'

The party leadership faced a stark choice. It could go ahead with the planned protest on 2 November. But now it seemed riskier and riskier. With their dwindling numbers, the leaders felt they would soon be overwhelmed. Khan had not yet gone out of his residence, apprehensive that his arrest could throw the party's protest awry.

But now the concern was, what would happen if Khan got arrested? Would there be enough outcry and reaction from the rest of the public? Would they pour out in massive numbers against Khan's arrest? The sudden realization was that it was a gamble the party could not take.

There was another factor, a decisive factor.

The party was 'also counting on the tension that has been playing out between the government and the military', Ejaz Haider, a prominent political analyst and talk show host, said.

In the August 2014 political standoff, Khan and Tahir-ul Qadri's supporters clashed violently with police, especially when they tried to enter the Prime Minister's Office. At that time, the military issued a warning in a press statement, urging the feuding sides to resolve their differences. One detail was telling. The military warned the government: 'Further use of force will only aggravate the problem.'

That warning then tied the hands of the civilian government.

But this time, there was no such indication from the military. No press statement followed the Swabi clashes between PTI and police.

The silence of the military—the absence of any public messaging against the police and paramilitary crackdown—suggested that the army would not be drawn into the conflict, despite the wishes of many.

It also made clear to the PTI leadership and the fence-sitters, both in public and political circles, that the party did not have the overt support of the military.

Khan realized that dragging out the confrontation any longer was pointless. Now it was time to climb down. The government had already offered face-saving. The military also seemed to favour a solution through the Supreme Court.

'The Supreme Court's decision to form a commission of inquiry, determine its Terms of reference, and begin hearings expeditiously came as a face-saver for PTI,' said Haider. 'And, to a lesser extent, for the government.'

By the afternoon of 1 November, Khan again appeared before the cameras, wearing the traditional *shalwar qameez*, and announced calling off the protest.

Now, it was time for Khan to give the retreat a spin. It was time to declare that the apparent defeat was a victory and to reveal to the crowds that not only was he the country's greatest cricket captain, but he was also its greatest political strategist.

Chapter 11

The New Army Chief

November 2016

Prime Minister Nawaz Sharif ended months of speculation as he announced his choice of Lt Gen. Qamar Javed Bajwa as the new army chief.

Gen. Bajwa, an infantry soldier, is thought of as a strict believer in civilian supremacy and has an enlightened, liberal outlook, according to those who know him personally. The army general also believes that, apart from India, non-state actors are the biggest threat to the country. These convictions of the army chief-designate must have leant heavily on the mind of Prime Minister Nawaz Sharif as he made the crucial appointment.

The prime minister kept his cards close to his chest, delaying the announcement till the very end as he gave the outgoing army chief, Gen. Raheel Sharif, a cordial and dignified sendoff. Prime Minister Nawaz Sharif used the last few weeks to effectively discredit all the self-proclaimed military representatives in the media and assert that the buck stops with him.

The outgoing chief, Gen. Raheel Sharif, enjoyed immense, unprecedented popularity, and it cast a long shadow over the civilian government, leading to big perceptions of a parallel power structure. The huge imbalance in civil–military relations has been a constant source of friction between the two power structures.

With Gen. Bajwa's elevation, the prime minister hopes to balance the heavily tilted civil-military equation, his aides said. How far the new chief remains faithful to his convictions of civilian supremacy remains to be seen, given the overarching influence of the military and its control of security and foreign policies.

As per usual practice, after assuming charge, Gen. Bajwa will shuffle key appointments as he brings his team to the fore.

Gen. Bajwa will continue the operations against non-state actors within the country with the same vigour exhibited by his predecessor. The new chief's extensive knowledge of the Kashmir frontier and the Line of Control, which has heated up in recent months, will also be invaluable as hostilities with India rise to a sharp new dimension. Gen. Bajwa had earlier served as the corps commander of X Corps, which is stationed in Rawalpindi and deals with Kashmir.

Lt. Gen. Zubair Mahmood Hayat, the newly appointed Chairman of the Joint Chiefs of Staff Committee, was always thought to be the best choice for the post. Unlike popular perception, the CJCSC is not just a ceremonial position. CJSC controls the Strategic Plans Division, which is the secretariat of the National Command Authority and manages all aspects of the country's nuclear, missile, and space programmes. Gen. Hayat was already the director-general for the Strategic Plans Division for a short stint and was then posted to the all-important position of chief of the general staff, which is second only to the army chief.

The other two contenders for army chief were Lt Gen. Ashfaq Nadeem and Lt Gen. Javed Iqbal Ramday. Lt Gen. Nadeem has as impressive a military resume as you can get. But his hard-charging reputation and the impression that he was Gen. Raheel's preferred choice were his undoing. Lt Gen. Ramday had close family links with the Sharifs, and despite that comfort level, there was an enormous political cost to pay if he was elevated. A political government already embroiled in a lingering political crisis could not afford to provide further ammunition to its political opponents, apart from creating an even more unfavourable impression within the military.

Chapter 12

The Army Chief's Vow: Coordination, Not Competition, with Civilians

November 2016

The gathering of senior army officers from Rawalpindi Garrison sat alert in the General Headquarters auditorium and listened to their chief intently. It was the last week of December, and Gen. Qamar Javed Bajwa, the army chief, had been promoted to the top job just weeks earlier. The general delivered his first speech—an articulation of his vision—as the new army chief in a poised manner and communicated it to his officers in unequivocal terms. The army has no business trying to run the government, the general said. The army must remain within its constitutionally defined role, he stressed.

Gen. Bajwa also alluded to the fact that the impression of competition between civilians and the military is counterproductive for the country. And, apart from other professional advice, he urged officers to read the book *Army and Nation* written by Steven I. Wilkinson.

The almost 300-page book makes for an interesting read as it details why the democratic process in India has been a success. Wilkinson, a professor of political science and international relations at Yale University, explores the command and control strategies, careful ethnic balancing, political and foreign policies and strategic decisions that made the army not interfere in Indian democracy.

Wilkinson argues that India took several steps after Partition to correct the civil–military imbalance. It greatly helped that the Indian Congress was a broad-based political party and better institutionalized than the Muslim League, which, in the first decade after Partition, was unable to provide political stability and legitimacy.

He further states that the military in India is also not seen as an attractive avenue of employment, unlike in the 1930s, when high officer salaries, land patronage, tax remissions and other incentives made the military a coveted career. India has reduced the roles of ethnic groups within its military, and no singular group threatens or overshadows the rest. After the 1962 war with China, India has been aggressive in trying to 'balance outside the army' with a huge increase in paramilitary forces. However, back here, Zulfiqar Ali Bhutto's attempt to raise a parallel paramilitary force, the Federal Security Force (FSF), failed.

Now that it has been a month since his ascension to the powerful position, it can be discerned that while Gen. Bajwa believes in civilian supremacy, he will also not do anything that upends those existing structures and dynamics. When a controversy broke out recently about land allocated to the former army chief, Gen. Raheel Sharif, a sharp, almost edgy, rebuttal came from the military.

However, the comparison between the personal styles of Gen. Raheel Sharif and Gen. Bajwa cannot be starker. While the previous army chief basked and glowed under the glare of television and press cameras, Gen. Bajwa likes to go about his job without pomp and show. His trips to the frontlines or speeches to troops have lacked the breathless coverage that was the defining factor of the former army chief's tenure. Till now, there has been no attempt to portray Gen. Bajwa as a parallel, competing powerhouse with strong political undertones, unlike in the past, when an orchestrated campaign was directed and aimed at raising the profile of the then army chief to mythic proportions. It cast a long shadow over the civilian leaders.

Through his public statements, Gen. Bajwa has stressed that the army will support and assist the civilian government in the national interest. 'United we rise' is the theme adopted by the military and its media wing under the leadership of the new army chief, officials say.

The civilians can draw comfort from these initial indicators and feel relieved that no efforts to destabilize the political system will emanate from the garrison city. But it should also not lull them into a false sense of security or complacency. The political system will get more strength and legitimacy from its own acts and conduct. Good governance, transparent accountability and zero tolerance for corruption—from top to bottom—are only the first steps towards a stable, democratic country that is not constantly threatened by the possibility of a military coup.

Chapter 13

Imran's Colourful Ally

February 2017

Beneath the clear sky on a lush green lawn of a house located in a posh neighbourhood of Islamabad, Sheikh Rashid Ahmed, a famous politician from Rawalpindi, stood while his two German Shepherds frolicked around. Recently, he moved to this secure residence, surrounded by towering walls and patrolled by guards.

In the driveway, behind another SUV snug in a car cover rested a bulletproof Land Cruiser. This new haven, he shared with a puff on his signature Cuban cigar, pointing towards the dwelling, was his 'sanctuary'.

The serenity of the manicured yard and the quiet leafy street stood in stark contrast to the bustling environment of the Rawalpindi constituency, which Sheikh Rashid, as he is colloquially known, represents. However, with the imminent threat of a militant attack looming over Lal Haveli, his pre-partition political headquarters, and the government accusing him of unauthorized occupancy of the building, with a deadline to vacate by 8 March, he found solace here.

Undaunted by the circumstances, Sheikh Rashid remarked, 'What's there to lose? I'm a political kamikaze.'

While he rebuffs the notion of conceding Lal Haveli, he has resolved to establish his alternative office in this house, with refurbishment operations still in progress in the upper portion.

As the Supreme Court continues to deliberate over the Sharif family's overseas wealth, the astute politician senses triumph. Being a constant presence in every court hearing, he compares himself to an assiduous student who never skips classes. 'I may not have been regular at school or college, but here, punctuality is paramount,' he stated, referring to the popularly known Panama case.

'This case is of paramount significance and will have a decisive impact on our country. I am a part of this history in the making. Whatever the verdict will be, it will be historic,' he said, lounging on the drawing room sofa.

The Panama Papers disclosures have rekindled the political prospects of both Sheikh Rashid and Khan, arch-enemies of Prime Minister Nawaz Sharif. Renowned for his astute political catchphrases, Rashid is candid about his past prophecies of the government's downfall. He stood by his 2014 declaration of a political sacrifice before Eidul Azha, the sacrificial feast, even as it circulated widely. 'The soldier failed to get in touch with me; I am unaware of the reason,' he said, alluding to the military.

With renewed conviction, he said, 'Regardless of the verdict, Nawaz Sharif's political image will take a hit.'

Sheikh Rashid envisages leveraging the Panama scandal till the elections if he can persuade Khan. Comparing the Panama Papers scandal to Richard Nixon's Watergate and the Bofors gun scandal, he stated his ambition to incite a similar movement.

The unpredictability of Khan's political demeanour is the only hurdle he faces. 'Khan listens to me, and I respect him,' he said. 'However, Khan has his political structure, his party, and his obligations.'

Sheikh Rashid grabbed nationwide attention last October when, despite police attempts to thwart him, he managed to reach the protest rally venue. A video of him gasping for breath as he navigated Rawalpindi's labyrinthine streets to evade the police became viral.

'Proudly I say that my 28 October motorbike show won their hearts, despite not having done anything for my constituency this time,' Sheikh Rashid's voice echoed, his face beaming.

With politics brimming with theatrics, Sheikh Rashid is no exception. He frequently cites his constituents' opinions in his public speeches. A testament to this is a story about a local samosa seller predicting Rashid's election victory, owing to his motorbike show.

Yet, he holds concerns for another Rawalpindi constituency, from which Khan won the previous election. 'Khan hasn't visited the constituency despite my suggestions, which presents me with a significant challenge,' he said.

Nevertheless, he remains hopeful that the Panama Papers case will aid him and has anchored his political strategy around this controversy. 'I have an undying love for politics, and I detest any indulgence in women, alcohol, or gambling,' he emphasized.

Referring to his political compatriot, Khan, he shared, 'Khan is a family man.' However, he expressed concern over Khan's wait for a marital commitment. 'I've often told him that there's a season for everything, and one should contemplate significantly before taking up bank employment or marrying at an old age,' he said.

As he eagerly awaits the upcoming Wednesday, another opportunity to appear before the Supreme Court judges in the Panama Papers case, Sheikh Rashid is prepared to present compelling evidence. Though he did not disclose any further details, he was confident that his proof would cause substantial political turmoil. 'It will be like a nuclear assault,' he proclaimed.

Chapter 14

A New Military Operation

Reflection of new ownership

February 2017

The media juggernaut of former army chief Gen. Raheel Sharif after the launch of Operation Zarb-e-Azb in 2014 left a powerful and lasting impact on the public imagination. The relative decline in terror attacks helped restore the military's image after the impression that it had dithered under Gen. Ashfaq Pervez Kayani. The period of peace provided relief to the terror-ravaged populace and catapulted Gen. Raheel Sharif's persona to new, dizzying heights.

On the other hand, the political government remained shaky and off-balanced due to the constant political campaign by Khan, the leader of PTI. The former army chief filled the resultant political vacuum and kept the government on its toes until he retired.

The critics maintained that much of the claims of victory were skewed versions of ground reality and glossed over by a careful and forceful media management campaign. The military did wean off most of the areas that were under terrorist control. But the real extent of the damage inflicted on militants remained unclear. The lull in armed violence, however, overshadowed these concerns.

The renewed militant violence this month has laid bare the efficacy of earlier claims. As suicide bombings rocked the main cities and targeted a revered shrine, questions bubbled up. Were initial claims hollow, or had the country sleepwalked back into the terror terrain?

Since the last quarter of 2016, various militant groups have been trying to form a coalition, setting aside their differences. Security officials say the militants have received a new injection of financial assistance to revive their activities; the traces lead to hostile foreign agencies that want to destabilize the country and stymie economic progress. The former army chief was lucky to escape the confluence of these developments and militants' blowback.

A sizeable portion of the public, under the influence of the media blitz, has a fervent desire for success in appearance, if not in reality. Inevitably, the public grew restless as recent terror attacks wrecked the country.

The feeling also filtered into the military's ranks and file. In the fast-changing circumstances, the new military leadership was forced to come forward to show that it was not trailing the successes claimed by its predecessors. The transmogrification of Operation Zarb-e-Azb into Operation Radd-ul-Fasaad is actually an indication of these factors. The rebranding and repackaging of military and intelligence operations are an announcement of new ownership under the new leadership.

The effectiveness of this new push against militant networks in urban and rural centres remains to be seen. The real thing to watch out for would be the impact of powers given to the paramilitary forces in Punjab, the political power base of the ruling Pakistan Muslim League. The Sharif brothers were earlier resistant to the idea of paramilitary troops fanning out across their province.

The difference added strain to the relationships between them and the top brass. But now, with the new realities and emerging dangers, the opposition was no longer sustainable. There was no choice for the ruling political party but to concede. Gradually, the Rangers will turn into an influential stakeholder in the power matrix of Punjab. There will not be any going back.

And the familiar tableau of civil-military balance or imbalance will also be re-enacted in the greater political realm.

Chapter 15

Panama Papers Court Verdict

21 April 2017

The air of anticipation over Courtroom No. 1 of the Supreme Court was so thick on 20 April that it could be cut with a knife. Opposition politicians and government ministers started arriving here right after 1 p.m. looking for seats that offered the best view. The courtroom was swarming with lawyers, young and old, as they elbowed political workers and journalists for space, even in the corners allocated for print media.

Jahangir Tareen arrived much earlier than Imran Khan and sat with Aleem Khan. Anusha Rehman, the minister for IT and Telecom, was shepherded by party loyalists to a front seat, where she sat pensively for under half an hour before the verdict announcement. Ahsan Iqbal and Khawaja Asif sat a few rows behind.

But it was Daniyal Aziz whose demeanour best reflected the ruling party's mood. Daniyal stood on the left corner of the court, chewing bubble gum nonchalantly. An obsequious lawyer, who was standing nearby, turned to the brash and vocal lawmaker, and said, 'You have lost weight. Have you started going to the gym?' Daniyal looked at the lawyer dismissively and said, 'No. It's the same.'

'You were smart earlier also, but now you have become smarter,' the lawyer continued. 'Not at all. We cannot spoil the name of the *Motu* Gang,' Daniyal said, making a self-deprecating joke ('motu' means 'fat' in Urdu), as others around him joined in the cackle.

The justices arrived at their seats as the clock struck 2 p.m. Before reading the order, Justice Asif Saeed Khosa asked those present in the court to respect the decorum and express their reactions outside the court. Justice Khosa said there was a 3–2 split in the verdict and said he and Justice Gulzar Ahmed were among the dissenters. It was not a surprise, as, during the court hearings, Justice Khosa had made several remarks that clearly showed his disbelief in the proofs cited by the lawyers of the prime minister.

There were no loud gasps or murmurs when Justice Khosa read the first part of the order, detailing the formation of a Joint Investigation Team to probe the ruling family's financial matters. It was in the later part when he read out his dissenting note, stating that the prime minister had failed to provide ample evidence and had been dishonest not only to the court but also to the nation, that a loud collective whisper erupted in the courtroom.

The PTI supporters wanted to hear it as the primary verdict and were immediately disappointed when they realized that the majority decision ruled out the removal of the prime minister from office. Khan sprang up from his seat and left the courtroom quickly, as the rest of his party members leapt after him. 'Anything short of a disqualification is a victory for us,' said a lawyer, ostensibly a PML–N supporter, loudly as he rushed towards the exit door.

At the doorsteps of the Supreme Court's entrance, there were already shouts of victory by the supporters of the PML–N.

Khan and other PTI leaders quickly slunk out of the court premises, evading the bevvy of microphones and cameras.

Naeem Bokhari, the counsel for Khan, who once famously remarked that lawyers never lose a case, only clients do, was also in a hurry to leave. 'In the country's history, such questions and remarks have never been given about a prime minister like the ones given regarding this prime minister,' Bokhari said when asked if the court verdict was a defeat of his party before the court.

He was wearing sunglasses, like most PTI leaders, but had taken off his black lawyer's jacket. 'If the Sharifs have any ounce of shame, they should leave for Anatolia,' he said with a laugh.

Chapter 16

Opposition Smells Blood in Water

23 April 2017

Since it is an open season to quote the French novelists and playwrights, especially Honore de Balzac, one is tempted to follow the vogue. Apart from casting doubt on the origins of all great fortunes and wealth, Balzac also remarked, 'Conscience is our unerring judge until we finally stifle it.'

Ever since the announcement of the Panama Papers verdict, many politicians and commentators have demanded the resignation of the prime minister on 'moral grounds'. Morals and conscience are the first casualties when an individual steps into the political arena. Stifling one's conscience is, therefore, the Faustian bargain of every politician. Calls for a resignation are politically naive and hopelessly idealistic. Prime Minister Nawaz Sharif will not throw in the towel.

The Panama Papers verdict could not have been different if one went by the law. All those who understood it and were not swayed by political emotions and ambitions anticipated that the Supreme Court could not shed away its essence of being an appellate court. The formation of an investigation panel, be it a judicial commission or a joint investigation team, was inevitable.

But even here, the justices have employed a perplexing method. There is stinging and scathing commentary and admonishment based on morality and, understandably, scepticism about the Sharif family's wealth. But tossing the investigation back to the same institutions, which received a damning critique from the justices in the verdict, is indeed akin to chewing their own words.

The inclusion of the military's intelligence officials is wrought with future complications. Flashes of populism and political bias are a tad bit evident in the dissenting notes. There is also the impression that the dissenting justices have attempted to increase the space and outreach of judicial powers. And since both dissenting justices will head the Supreme Court soon, the practical demonstration of this attempt is not too far away.

For the ruling family, the path forward will be downhill. The carefully crafted image of a hard-working, middle-class family, observant of religion and eastern traditional values, has been cracked. The consistent, year-long hullaballoo over the Panama Papers revelations has placed the ruling party in the same spot of public opprobrium that spurns corruption and has stuck like tar with the PPP.

Khan had sought the help of the military earlier and was now counting on justices to oust the Prime Minister. But PTI has now realized that it has no friends, and therefore, Khan's knee-jerk response has been to revert to the streets.

The increasing political agitation and dissent in the political arena are expected to put more pressure on Prime Minister Nawaz Sharif. The coming weeks will indicate how much momentum the anti-Nawaz sentiment gains.

Opposition politicians, especially Asif Ali Zardari, smell blood in the water. The former president realizes that Khan's politics run short on guile and remain high on rhetoric and social media optics. While PTI exhausts its energy in back-to-back rallies and street agitation, Zardari has embarked on reconnecting with politicians he thinks can win seats in the next elections.

Given the deep polarization and PML–N's diminishing position, the next parliament is expected to be a hung parliament. Even if the combined opposition forces an early election by the end of this year, the result will not be different.

For Prime Minister Nawaz Sharif, the choices are stark. With a slipping grip on power and a lack of widespread popularity, he cannot hope to win a majority in the next elections. Khan is continuously chipping away at his power base in Punjab and is expected to gain more strength. It makes political sense to strike a bargain now (yes, once again) with Asif Ali Zardari. But there is more likelihood of an intense three-way fight between Nawaz Sharif, Asif Ali Zardari and Khan until the elections.

Now that brand Nawaz Sharif has been tainted and the brand Maryam Nawaz Sharif got off to a hobbled start, there is a need to recalibrate. Will they be able to find a new incarnation after 'Panama Papers'? PML–N supporters are inclined to say, '*Inshallah!*'

Chapter 17

Army Chief and Prime Minister Defuse a Lingering Crisis

May 2017

The '*Dawn* Leaks' kerfuffle has ended in a dramatic—almost unimaginable—manner. For months, the frenzy over the so-called 'national security breach' dominated headlines and destabilized civil–military relations. This was even though army chief Gen. Qamar Javed Bajwa has repeatedly expressed his faith in democracy and his desire for civil–military harmony. However, as an institution, the pressures exerted by the rank and file appeared to eclipse the intentions of the chief. A section of the military pressured the army chief to hold the government accountable for the alleged national security breach.

But as the dust over the matter has started settling down, it has been revealed that the pressure originated from the coterie of the previous army chief, Gen. Raheel Sharif, who desired an extension to his military tenure. The controversy over the newspaper article presented the perfect opportunity to pin the prime minister down.

There has also been a steady stream of allegations, propagated by some in the media and elements of the 'Deep State', that have cast Prime Minister Nawaz Sharif as a security risk himself. Prime Minister Sharif's policy predilections towards India and personal friendships with an Indian business tycoon have fuelled the impression.

Furthermore, Maryam Nawaz Sharif, the heir to the Sharif political dynasty, has been the target of a vicious smear campaign. Rumours swirled loud and hard that it was she who masterminded the *Dawn* Leaks to embarrass and ridicule the military. Denials from the ruling family have done little to dilute this propaganda campaign.

However, the Joint Investigation Team probing the *Dawn* Leaks found no smoking gun that linked the first daughter to the leaks. Two close aides of the Prime Minister had to face the axe, and a senior bureaucrat was the collateral damage. But the notification from the Prime Minister's office last week was still deemed insufficient and consequently 'rejected' in the now infamous tweet.

Director General ISPR Major Asif Ghafoor, who headed the military's media wing at the time, said in a tweet:

'Notification on Dawn Leak is incomplete and not in line with recommendations by the Inquiry Board. Notification is rejected.'

The resultant political storm was inevitable. The opposition political parties lapped it up, relishing the prospect of a showdown between the military and the ruling party.

Prime Minister Nawaz Sharif, however, kept his nerves and continued with his visits across the country, inaugurating his signature development projects. The prime minister, despite the Panama Papers controversy, continues to enjoy considerable popular support, and he used the rallies to show his opponents, both in the establishment and political arena, that he will not be cowed down.

Meanwhile, the controversy over the Inter-Services Public Relations (ISPR) tweet and the strong social media reaction against it came as a surprise to the military establishment. The contrarian voices, critical of the tone of the tweet and its crossing of the constitutional line, were especially disconcerting.

The pressure on Prime Minister Nawaz Sharif could have become insurmountable had the political opposition been united or Khan, the leading player, been effective enough to create an unstable political situation. But Khan's followers suffer from attrition and are unable to mount a sustained campaign like the 2007 lawyers' movement.

So, while the anti-government anchors fumed and frowned on TV screens, creating a faux image of the government buckling down, in the realm of realpolitik, Prime Minister Nawaz Sharif still managed to withstand the pressure. Having sacrificed two of his close aides, the prime minister was unwilling to concede any further.

The ruling party sent out calculated media leaks and feelers that threw the gauntlet back at their challengers. The PML–N conveyed to the other side that now that a deadlock had emerged, the party was ready for the consequences. It was indicated that no new notification would be issued.

Meanwhile, there was a rethink on the part of Gen. Bajwa regarding the infamous tweet. The army chief and the director-general of Inter-Services Public Relations had taken a tough posture towards the government, pressed by comparisons with their predecessors, who basked in confrontational and overarching roles. It was also decided that at a time when security challenges at the eastern and western borders have suddenly flared up, continued political instability and a fractious political environment within the country would only exacerbate the challenges faced by the state.

Through backchannel negotiations and contacts, an understanding was reached. Both sides decided to take one step backwards to come out of the stalemate. Official sources say that the army chief, Gen. Qamar Javed Bajwa, and Prime Minister Nawaz Sharif agreed to 'uphold the sanctity of all institutions' and not allow the current crisis to bring the entire system down. The government agreed to issue a notification, through the interior ministry, that detailed steps be taken following the findings of the inquiry report. The military agreed to take the tweet back, calling it 'infructuous'.

Chapter 18

Last Eid with 'Prime Minister' Nawaz Sharif?

June 2017

The speculation windmill in political circles and whispers in the power corridors of Islamabad and Rawalpindi are suddenly in sync: the fate of Prime Minister Nawaz Sharif's stay in power is sealed because of the proceedings of the probe of the Joint Investigation Team constituted by the Supreme Court.

It is just a matter of weeks now, they say.

More than a year after the revelations in the so-called Panama Papers rattled the globe and forced several political leaders to resign, Sharif's attempts to forestall the inevitable seem to have come to nought. Earlier this year, the Supreme Court justices stopped short of removing the Prime Minister, but it was evident from the formation of the probe team, comprising civil and military investigators, that the cards were heavily stacked against the Prime Minister. The ruling party's media spokespersons tried desperately to paint the proceedings as biased and predetermined. Leaks allegedly coming from the investigators added to the widespread perception that the ruling family had failed to account for their overseas wealth.

Over the weekend, Nawaz Sharif appeared before a coterie of familiar and preferred journalists in London and reiterated his old defence. The probe against his family was nothing more than a political witch-hunt and personal vendetta of his opponents, the prime minister said with a visibly sullen face. 'The real JIT will be the 2018 elections,' he said in what sounded like conceding defeat even before the probe team has furnished its findings to the Supreme Court.

If the premonitions of the ruling party and indications from the JIT are any measure, the Supreme Court will hold Sharif unfit to rule by the end of this month. And, thereafter, we are heading into a time of political tumult and political uncertainty.

The ruling Pakistan Muslim League can either choose a new prime minister or call for snap elections. However, the probability of the PML–N calling for a national vote before the Senate elections remains low. Even though Sharif seemed predisposed to an adverse Supreme Court ruling, he nonetheless expressed the resolve to put up a determined fight.

Several names are being tossed around for the interim Prime Minister, including Ahsan Iqbal, who is on good terms with the military establishment and the Chinese, and Khurram Dastgir-Khan, a soft-spoken politician with an untainted reputation.

The problem for the 'powers to be' is that even if Prime Minister Nawaz Sharif is ousted, the political entity of Nawaz Sharif cannot be just wiped off. The former army chief, Pervez Musharraf, could not manage to do so despite having a strong ten-year grip on power. How will the current string pullers—who rely on electronic media leaks and social media trends—ensure erasing PML–N from the political landscape?

That hope is a comforting thought for the current ruling party as it contemplates entering the elections under Maryam Nawaz Sharif and Shehbaz Sharif's leadership in a post-Nawaz as Prime Minister scenario.

For Khan, the removal of Nawaz Sharif as the Prime Minister will undoubtedly come as a huge moral and political victory. Through dogged persistence and unwavering determination,

Imran Khan kept hammering the Panama Papers scandal into the national psyche. It is also a fact that some elements of the Deep State provided a cushion for Imran's constant and sometimes dwindling efforts.

But the real challenge for the PTI leader is to convert this political victory into an electoral one. The recent rush by some politicians is indicative of a realization by some that holding a Pakistan People's Party (PPP) ticket in the national elections is a kiss of death. Asif Ali Zardari's efforts to keep his crumbling party in order have met with failure, forcing him to leave the country shortly after the much-trumped-up attempts to revive the party.

Also, the establishment nudged some politicians to join PTI as it tried to tip the balance of power. Imran Khan will gain a major chunk of votes in Punjab, but the PTI remains hobbled by its lack of organization in Sindh and Balochistan.

A hung parliament, therefore, seems inevitable in the current political calculus.

While the Panama Papers scandal is expected to end Sharif's reign, it remains unclear what institutional mechanisms against systemic and endemic corruption in the state machinery will emerge from this political struggle. Will it usher the country into a new dawn of accountability and transparency or drag it further into power struggles and backroom intrigues?

If Sharif remains the only casualty and other civilian and former military rulers escape accountability, the whole struggle of the past year will lose its shine and sheen. The 2007 Lawyers Movement ended up just restoring Iftikhar Muhammad Chaudhry as the chief justice and removing Pervez Musharraf from power but fell terribly short of all other vaunted promises of reform and change.

The current political struggle risks the same fate.

Chapter 19

The Contractor

July 2017

Raymond Davis's book *The Contractor: How I Landed in a Pakistani Prison and Ignited a Diplomatic Crisis* has opened a can of worms. It has resulted in political and personal point-scoring and institutional sniping. Much of the initial reaction here has been about the role of ISI and, more specifically, about Lt Gen. Ahmad Shuja Pasha (retd). The former spy chief is being criticized, especially on social media, for orchestrating and micromanaging a deal with the Americans that saw the release of Davis from a prison in Lahore.

Gen. Pasha was a spy chief, unlike his predecessors. He had no mystery about him. Unlike some former ISI chiefs, Gen. Pasha came with no prior experience in intelligence, be it in the ISI or Military Intelligence (MI). He was catapulted to the powerful DG I position from that of director-general military operations (DGMO). And Gen. Pasha did not try to cultivate the air of mystique, inaccessibility, or authority exerted through behind-the-scenes manoeuvring. He came out in the open and, in the process, overexposed himself. His interactions with politicians and journalists were far greater than those of his predecessors and far more widely reported.

While eloquence was one of his strengths, he was prone to sudden oscillations between emotional outbursts and steely threats. His engagements and conversations usually had one consistent theme: civilians were neither patriotic nor capable, and, worst of all, they were corrupt and easy sellouts.

The revelation that the steely Gen. Pasha, who took no time to steamroll the locals, had a different attitude towards the Americans is bound to rankle those who have suffered on his side.

Pakistani officials sometimes say different things to different audiences. In some cases, it may be necessary. But the truth of the matter is that while addressing the local audience, the tone of the officials is stern, harsh, and even admonishing. The same tone becomes soft and ingratiating when meeting with Western officials, especially from the US.

Many critics have expressed shock over the disclosure of Gen. Pasha's role and minute details about how he texted the Americans with regular updates while sitting through the court proceedings of the Davis trial. But blaming Gen. Pasha as solely responsible for having cut a deal with the Americans is also misplaced. Gen. Pasha did not work independently of his boss Gen. Kayani.

There is a very revealing US diplomatic cable in Wikileaks in which an American diplomat notes how both generals appeared to work in tandem. While Gen. Kayani would maintain his quiet posture, Gen. Pasha was all expression. (The relations between the two only turned sour towards the end of Pasha's second tenure as DGI, when Gen. Kayani even stopped taking his calls.)

The decision to release Raymond Davis had the approval of Gen. Kayani and the military as an institution. The civilians did not really have much say in the mechanics of the release. At best, the civilians wanted to not have to deal with the issue. It is, therefore, strange that Gen. Pasha is now claiming, through the vessel of Lt Gen. Amjad Shoaib (retd), that the decision was taken only after and due to the civilian consensus and that he was acting merely as an enforcer.

The good old general should take responsibility. If the decision to release Davis was taken in the interest of the state and the greater regional geostrategic situation, it must be presented that way.

Some people are also suggesting that the timing of the book is rooted in a psyops campaign by the Americans and point to the sudden, free-of-charge proliferation of the book within the country as proof. But it is also true that it does not take much to propagate and promote content through WhatsApp. Anyone downloading the e-version and passing it on could have triggered a mass chain of propagation of the book.

The account by Raymond Davis is certainly slanted and self-serving; on many occasions, it is condescending and demeaning to not only the military but also to the Pakistani people. But it also throws a spotlight on the relations between Pakistan and the United States and the interactions of officials. It is an American lens through which the country is being viewed and presented. The book should be read in that context. The military will not gain much if it dismisses the book as just propaganda and an excuse to lambast the civilians further. The civilians are also off the mark when they vent at Gen. Pasha for a deal that was expedient for both countries.

Chapter 20

Supreme Court Fires Nawaz Sharif

July 2017

The Supreme Court dealt a stunning blow to Nawaz Sharif as it went full throttle and ordered his removal from office apart from the initiation of criminal proceedings against the three children, the son-in-law and Ishaq Dar. Many did not expect such a damning and wide-ranging verdict, which has spectacularly tilted the political equilibrium.

After all, the powerful have always managed to escape accountability in the country's checkered history. And Nawaz Sharif, the powerful and mighty politician who has ruled over Punjab for over three decades, seemed untouchable until just last year. He had managed to withstand the two attempts at a putsch by Khan, his main political nemesis, during the infamous 2014 Islamabad siege and 2016 lockdown. He managed to smoothly transition out of the overarching and overbearing army chief, Gen. Raheel Sharif. And when Gen. Qamar Javed Bajwa took the cane of command, many in the ruling party celebrated. A hostile general no longer heads ISI. The brewing controversy over the revelations of the Panama Papers seemed more like an itch than a fatal wound. What could go wrong?

But as 2017 rolled forward and court proceedings wound down, Nawaz Sharif looked increasingly vulnerable. The legal defence was a shambles, if not ludicrous. The political response to the compelling narrative of Khan has been meek. And such has been the political tumult over the bruising investigation of the Joint Investigation Team that the Sharif family found it almost impossible to recover. No amount of forewarnings about conspiracies, both local and international, has provided comfort. And, within the corridors of power in the capital and neighbouring Rawalpindi, whispers about the impending ouster of Nawaz Sharif have started to get louder and louder.

Still, many hoped that the justices would not go all the way. Nawaz Sharif's supporters have pointed to the unusual behaviour of the bench, the lack of legal precedents, and the inability of the investigative team to directly link him with the London apartments.

The fact that a trial had not been completed added to their optimism. But the bench, it seems, had made up its mind from the onset.

There is also reason to believe that the powerful military establishment gave a tacit, if not overt, nod as the court reached the moment of the final announcement.

And, with one swift stroke, the court has shafted the Sharif family.

While Nawaz Sharif remains disqualified to hold public office in the foreseeable future, it remains to be seen how much damage has been done to the political entity that is Nawaz Sharif and its political representation, the PML–N. The party attempted hard to discount any impressions of a crack or a fissure. The challenge is to hold the party together and not let it fragment, as there are possibilities of defections and forward blocs emerging.

Maryam Nawaz Sharif, who is implicated in a long legal battle and risks herself being barred from public office, posted pictures of her smiling and relaxed father.

Other party leaders tried to sound defiant. 'We will make a comeback,' Khawaja Saad Rafique said. He taunted Khan as a 'mere pawn' in the greater political game. But it is also apparent that the party does not want to adopt a confrontational posture anymore. 'We will not ridicule the Supreme Court,' Shahid Khaqan Abbasi said. Khawaja Saad Rafique said the party would respect the institutions. 'There will be no chaos,' he added.

As PML–N chooses the next prime minister, Shehbaz Sharif most likely, it wants the transition to happen smoothly. The political future of the PML–N hinges on its ability to make it to the elections with infrastructure and energy projects completed. It cannot afford any more disruption.

Shehbaz Sharif's move to the capital does complicate things a little for the PML–N. The younger Sharif has maintained a strong grip over Punjab and was instrumental in the last General Election's win in the province. How effective would his successor be, and how would the bigwigs and heavyweights of local Punjab politics rally around Shehbaz Sharif's replacement?

Khan, the man who started it all and the main adversary of Nawaz Sharif, on the other hand, sounded strangely low-key in his press conference. Some people commented that he made the victory speech with the expressions of a defeated soldier. There was no exuberance. His voice lacked the usual tenor, and his uninhibited body language was slightly constricted. Is it that the great Khan—the slayer of Nawaz Sharif—now fears being undone by articles 61 and 62 of the Constitution? Already, there has been some talk about the Minus Two, or even 'Minus Three', formula (which suggested the disqualification of other leading politicians) in political circles.

The military has remained quiet all this time. The generals have never been comfortable with Nawaz Sharif and have spurned his insistence on 'civilian supremacy'. Furthermore, Nawaz Sharif's foreign-policy preferences were anathema to the core beliefs of the military, which is already wary about the encirclement of the country by hostile foreign powers. They stepped back over the *Dawn* Leaks issue, but it was only a tactical retreat.

In the greater realm of strategy, Nawaz was always an obstacle—a tainted, tarred politician who had to be done away with. And nothing could be better when the court itself was too keen to be used as the cat's paw.

Chapter 21

The Final Round

Political environment to get messier

December 2017

The political turmoil in the country has reached a new level. The latest voice adding to the state of uncertainty was that of National Assembly Speaker Ayaz Sadiq, who expressed his scepticism about the completion of parliament's term. The speaker alluded to some 'greater plan' at work that will send the assemblies packing. His television interviews were full of grave and sombre apprehensions but lacked specifics about the exact nature of the threat that stares at parliament. Cynics could portray the interviews as planted and poorly crafted—an unconvincing cry-wolf. But Sadiq had calculated that this was the best form of political messaging.

Some analysts, like Ayaz Amir, have questioned the very existence of any such 'greater plan' by the military. It seems that after ensuring that the court ousts Nawaz Sharif, the alleged planners of the military–judicial establishment have been a bit out of their wits. Instead of going for the kill soon after Nawaz Sharif's disqualification, they watched from the sidelines as Nawaz managed to raise his political profile, portray himself as a victim, and strengthen his hold over the party. The plan to install Shehbaz Sharif in the centre failed due to the manoeuvring of the elder brother and the lack of a visible push by the establishment.

Now, the PML–N government is limping and hobbling but still carrying on. It is another matter that inside the parliament, it is struggling to even maintain a simple quorum, or the legislation about delimitations and Federally Administered Tribal Area (FATA) is currently proving to be elusive, or the functioning of the bureaucracy in the secretariat is almost at a standstill. The collapse of the PML–N as a political party soon after Nawaz Sharif's disqualification simply did not happen.

It, however, has not dissuaded Sheikh Rashid, the eternal prophet of doom. The politician from Rawalpindi is convinced that the government will be toppled before March. Khan, the eternal harbinger of change, is galloping around the country and asking for early elections.

While some ministers in the government are making grim predictions about an extended caretaker setup in case the parliament does get dissolved early next year, Khan loses the most if a caretaker set-up comes into play for the next two to three years. It is therefore improbable to understand why he would put his weight behind such a dispensation unless there is something more than meets the eye and has been agreed upon with the grand planners. Khan's best bet is to force an early election and hope that he can rally the electorate around his mantra of corruption and governance. Some in the PTI are strongly advocating resigning from the national and Khyber Pakhtunkhwa assemblies to buckle down the government. Outside PTI, there are few takers for this gamble, and PPP is proving to be the most reluctant about this idea.

And it is obvious that Imran's politicking has not proven to be the Achilles heel of Nawaz Sharif. Instead, Nawaz Sharif is even more defiant, and his voter base in Punjab has been energized after he deftly played the victim card. Meanwhile, Maryam Nawaz Sharif has established her credentials as a potential leader.

Last month's protest sit-in at Faizabad, which was led by Maulana Khadim Rizvi, a firebrand cleric of the Barelvi sect and leader of the TLP religious group, is being viewed as the latest calibration by the military establishment in its effort to drive wedges in the traditional PML–N vote bank. But the high-handed way the agreement was brokered and the unusual, unprecedented way the name of a serving general was put on the agreement has resulted in more institutional embarrassment and international humiliation than a lasting sense of overcoming a national crisis. The workings of the 'internal wing' are being questioned in some quarters of the establishment.

By Friday evening, the decision about Khan and Jahangir Tareen's disqualification cases would be announced by the Supreme Court. If the courts decided to disqualify Jahangir Tareen, it would create space for Shah Mahmood Qureshi and the dark horse Asad Umar to become even more central to PTI's decision-making.

On the other hand, and more importantly, if Khan gets disqualified, it would really rattle the political environment and indicate that the establishment is surely at work to take out prominent politicians one by one. Next in line would be Asif Ali Zardari.

However, if Imran Khan gets a clean chit, it will breathe new life into the PTI's cadre and swing more of the fence-sitters towards the party. The PML–N will try to capitalize on such a verdict as an illustration of one-sided accountability. The politics will get even messier, and it will give the establishment the room it needs to manoeuvre.

Chapter 22

Nawaz Prepares for a Return

July 2018

The homecomings of political leaders are always dramatic and riveting. In September 2007, Nawaz Sharif was briefly arrested at Islamabad International Airport and bundled back to exile in Saudi Arabia after he made the first attempt to return to the country and challenge the then-military ruler, Gen. Pervez Musharraf. In November 2007, Nawaz managed to return to the country, and in the subsequent 2008 elections, the PML–N managed to retake Punjab, its traditional power base.

This time, in 2018, high drama once again awaits the three-time former prime minister and convicted politician as he returns to Lahore from a brief stay in London. However, the stakes are much higher for Nawaz Sharif compared to more than a decade ago.

The legacy and political future of not only the Sharif family but of the entire political party, PML–N, hang in a perilous balance. Unlike in 2007, Nawaz Sharif has lost much of the support and sympathy of international powers and backroom negotiators. Locally, a vast swath of the population reviles the Sharif family as the epitome of corruption and malfeasance.

The confrontation of the Sharifs with the security establishment has also become institutional. Back in 2007, only Gen. Musharraf and his close coterie were seen to be at loggerheads with Nawaz Sharif and his political party. However, now the mutual mistrust and acrimony have seeped further, with poisonous underpinnings. The differences have become irreconcilable, and the hatred has solidified.

Maryam Nawaz, the preferred political heiress of the ousted prime minister, is as determined and resolute in turning the page in the civil–military imbalance as the security establishment is intent on ensuring to snuff out her political career. The decision of the father–daughter duo to return to Pakistan and face jail, shunning the advice of going into exile for a few years, has, therefore, turned their political struggle into a final cataclysmic battle.

Nawaz Sharif is hoping for a sea of people to welcome him at Lahore Airport on Friday evening. The plan is to surrender to the National Accountability Bureau after a rousing speech. However, 'the powers that be' plan to steal Nawaz's thunder and intend to shift him and Maryam to Adiala Jail in Rawalpindi soon after they step onto the tarmac. PML–N is hoping for some showdowns with the police and security forces outside Lahore airport. The pictures and footage of such a highly charged political moment and scuffle are bound to reenergize the party's base. Images from Adiala prison would also send a powerful message to the party workers, who have been low on morale and confused about the dichotomy of political messages from Nawaz Sharif and Shehbaz Sharif. Nawaz Sharif and Maryam inside Adiala and Shehbaz Sharif and Hamza out on the campaign trail might save the party from sinking entirely.

The military has rejected allegations of political engineering ahead of the elections. However, such denials and clarifications will not allay the concerns of the PML–N and other political parties, except for PTI. Candidates have spoken about pressure, threatening phone calls, and summons to safe houses. Such allegations cannot be wished away or ignored.

Talk to the military officials, and from their perspective, the continuous cacophony over its overarching role in the civilian domain sounds hollow and self-serving. The military has evolved and gone through testing and challenging times in the last ten to fifteen years, the officers assert. The present-day generals and soldiers have not just stood guard at the borders. Each one of them has seen deaths and life-changing injuries too closely and has fought the militants too intensely in the tribal regions. They ask, how can it be that their sacrifices are not acknowledged? How can it be that the soldiers who were martyred or maimed in action did it for personal glory and not for the nation? Is it hegemonic to ask for honest and financially impeccable political leadership?

Such a line of reasoning and questioning would have found quick takers had the preferred alternates to PML–N not been cut from the same cloth. The preferred substitutes lack credibility and are dependent on the same set of 'electables', who have been the bane of Pakistani politics for decades. The pace of accountability has been lightning-fast in the case of the Sharifs. It has been blatantly selective in the application of the law across the board. The apparent synchronization of the courts and the security establishment cannot be just a simple coincidence.

Moreover, even though Chaudhry Nisar Ali Khan and Director-General Inter-Services Public Relations Maj. Gen. Asif Ghafoor both tried to distance themselves from the controversy over Jeep as an election symbol, the coincidences are too many and too uncanny. This is partly the reason Nawaz Shairf and Maryam have managed to find holes in the narrative parried by the politicians seen as close to or pliant to the security establishment.

PTI, on the other hand, now has a steady pace. Khan, the prime ministerial hopeful, is hopping from one campaign stop to another with confidence and ease. He feels encouraged by the idea that both natural and supernatural forces are on his side.

The response and reception Nawaz Sharif gets Friday will determine much of the momentum with which PML–N will go into the election. Nawaz knows that he is on the brink, and he will push the limits. His adversaries will push back in the same manner. It is never a good sign when the covers of intelligence operatives are blown or when the names of generals holding powerful portfolios in the intelligence apparatus become household names or get embroiled in political controversies.

The gloves had come off long ago. Now, there will be a fistfight.

Chapter 23

Election Day: 2018 Elections to Change Pakistan like Never Before

July 2018

It has been one hell of a ride. The political tumult and instability of the past couple of years were dizzying. The run-up to the election was incredibly messy and controversial. The spate of attacks hung like a dark, ominous cloud over the campaign trail. Allegations of meddling and 'political engineering' have already robbed today's would-be winner of some of the sweet taste of victory. However, the fact that Pakistanis will exercise their right to vote, and the country will complete its second democratic transition is nonetheless a positive sign.

Whether Imran Khan and the passionate supporters of PTI finally manage to win the national election will be known by late evening today.

Winning a thumping majority would be nothing but a spectacular and stunning victory for the former world-famous cricketer-turned-politician, who writhed in the political wilderness for decades. The widespread impression that the 'powers that be' have fixed the match for Imran Khan has not bothered his supporters. A vast swathe of the urban, educated middle-class population has blindly pinned hopes on 'the Captain'.

The burden of expectation and the desire for change are tremendous. Fulfilling these dreams and aspirations will not be easy. Governance is not a cakewalk in a country like Pakistan. The challenges staring at today's winner are staggering. A massive economic crisis is just around the corner. Geopolitical compulsions add to the complexity. The civil–military imbalance is a reality.

Those who expect that the removal of either of the two mainstream political parties from the power scene will miraculously solve the country's myriad of problems are in for a rude surprise. However, obstacles and impossibilities have never dimmed the idealism and passion of Khan's supporters.

The former ruling party, PML–N, is battered and bruised. The gruelling confrontation with the security establishment has been ugly and debilitating. However, the return of Nawaz Sharif and Maryam Nawaz Sharif did infuse new energy and lift the morale of the party. PML–N has remained resilient and defied expectations of falling like a pack of cards once Nawaz Sharif was ousted and barred from holding public office. Whether PML–N manages to defy further hopes of an electoral defeat in its heartland will become evident after the vote count is announced. Punjab's voter has spurned picking a fight with the establishment in the past, and traditionally, the Pakistani voter has opted to go with the side that looks to be winning. Will Punjab overturn this impression and go with the underdog? This has remained one of the most intriguing aspects of the current election.

The campaign trail saw the emergence of Bilawal Bhutto Zardari as a bright political prospect. He sounded humane and empathetic. He resisted mixing his political messaging with abuse and vitriol. He did not shy away from going through the grind and grime of campaigning. Bilawal, as a member of the parliament, will be someone to watch out for. The PPP is picking up pieces from the gigantic mess it turned into back in 2008. However, it has a long way to go to reclaim its past glory.

While continuity of democracy, no matter how hobbled, should be welcomed, concerns about growing sets of regulations, which feel like censorship, are mounting. The overarching role of the security establishment has received much criticism. The military has vigorously denied the allegations. Let us hope that the next government is not caught in the vicious circle of civil–military tensions and power games.

Even though Imran Khan failed to create the kind of wave that had catapulted him before the 2013 General Election, his party retains a fair chance of emerging as the single largest party. Having an absolute majority will make things easier for Khan. However, all bets are off if an alliance has to be stitched up.

The crisis of legitimacy is likely to affect the 2018 General Elections in ways far worse than the controversy of the 2013 votes. Whoever wins the election will quickly realize that the winner's crown is made of nothing but barbwire.

Section II
(2018–2022)

*The Hybrid Experiment Begins and Falters: Imran Khan as
Prime Minister and PTI's Handling of the Government*

Chapter 24

Come the Revolution

2 December 2018

Last week marked the completion of a hundred days of the PTI political party in office. Given the country's endemic structural problems and dysfunction, expecting the party, a first-time entrant in the corridors of power, to pull a miracle in just over three weeks is delusional. It is also understandable that PTI would term the last three months a resounding success, and its detractors would portray the government's performance as an abysmal failure. What is essential to analyse is whether the direction PTI has taken for reforms and governance looks promising or not.

The initial signs do not inspire much confidence. The government stumbled from one gaffe to another, from one embarrassing episode to the next. Most of the ministers have looked terribly out of their depth when it comes to performing their primary jobs and have been immensely talented and qualified to be hostile and sarcastic towards critics. The bureaucracy is petrified to sign any documents lest it become an excuse for the National Accountability Bureau to rake it over coals. Political statements have been hailed as transformative policies. Political somersaults have been described as a great strategy.

Government officials are incensed at the latest wave of criticism. What they fail to grasp is that people expected them to produce new and innovative solutions and not repackage the old ideas and economic and foreign policies of past governments.

Prime Minister Khan has now directed his ire at those with 'colonised minds'. Finance Minister Asad Umar has baulked at those who speak English with an affected accent. Some other officials have mocked those who throng the upscale eateries at Kohsar Market in the capital and M.M. Alam Road in the provincial capital, Lahore. The chickens are finally coming home to roost (pun intended).

The finance minister, Asad Umar, has been a peculiar revelation. His transformation from a corporate executive to a populist politician—high on rhetoric and low on substance—is now almost complete. His speech at the 100-day ceremony in Islamabad was telling. It was as little about finance as it was high on nationalist sentimentality, religious sentimentality and political grandstanding. It was as if he were pitching to be the next prime minister, and cynics could also conclude that he was trying to overshadow the prime minister, who was sitting right in front. No wonder there was some unease among those present in the audience.

Two generations have grown up idolizing Imran Khan. The cult and celebrity status of the prime minister is unmatched compared with any other local celebrity or politician. It helped catapult Khan to power and get away with what other mortals would have found politically fatal. He has managed to defy all criticism and achieve his ambitions with resolute single-mindedness.

It is still too early to tell whether this indomitable trait will help him overcome the daunting challenge he has set himself. However, the fact remains that he cannot pull it off alone this time. He would need much more than the constant mantra about corruption and the mishmash of varying, often contradictory economic models, and governance structures. Many of his idealistic notions have already clashed with stark realities. The expatriate Pakistanis have not started investing back in the country in bulk. Remittances have not skyrocketed. Moreover, having an honest man at the top does not stop or prevent the power politics of the mid-tier from playing it dirty and nasty.

Prime Minister Khan will have to make some course corrections soon and discard the extra baggage. He might want to gloss over some poor political choices and portray some visibly failing officials as beacons of change. It will not work. Within a year, some bad decisions will only compound and make matters worse. The prime minister can sound earnest and reassuring when he tells the public not to fret over the current rate of inflation, dipping value of the local currency and disappointing performance.

The constituents who helped ease the way for Khan to become the prime minister have been watching the initial bungling of the government with unease. They are still hopeful about their political choice. If the indicators of the much-anticipated economic turnaround still look grim within a year, their patience will be tested.

To the government's advantage, the opposition is in disarray. Despite their numerical strength in both houses of parliament, the combined opposition has failed to put the government on the defensive. The government's aggressive media strategy has been effective. The opposition leaders have themselves to blame. Sycophants and non-political advisors 'egged on' Nawaz Sharif and Maryam Nawaz, leading to a dead end. Now, their supporters feel abandoned in a no man's land while the Sharifs maintain a conspicuous, defeated silence. The slogan '[g]ive sanctity to my vote' sounds like a sad, discarded joke.

Chapter 25

A Unique Prime Minister

Imran Khan enjoys enduring goodwill despite a hobbled start

15 December 2018

Prime Minister Khan received a standing ovation as he walked in to attend the Defence and Martyrs Day ceremony at the GHQ earlier in September. Imran Khan had taken the oath as the Prime Minister just a few weeks ago and was basking in the glow of his electoral win.

When Gen. Qamar Javed Bajwa, the army chief, invited the new Prime Minister to address the ceremony, for a moment, Khan seemed unprepared. The start of the extempore speech was slightly awkward, but Imran Khan soon recovered as he spoke about his dream of strengthening the institutions, promoting merit and eliminating corruption.

The audience—mostly military families—burst into loud applause. Those in attendance seemed to have paid little attention to the imperfect start of an important speech at an event known for its formality, preparation, and decorum. There was an abiding air of goodwill for the new prime minister.

Fast forward a couple of months, and that sense of goodwill for Khan has endured. His popularity has not dipped; the charisma that has awed two generations shows no sign of fading. It does not seem to matter that the government's initial days seemed hobbled and directionless. Or that most of the cabinet ministers were found bumbling, and the criticism over the handling of the economy hung heavily, like a dark cloud, over the first hundred days in office.

Anyone else would have found the cacophony of criticism and the political opposition's loud condemnations daunting and unnerving.

Imran Khan, on the other hand, seems impervious and unscathed by the barrage of criticism.

More importantly, the faith of those who elected Khan to office remains strong. The confidence of the civil and military bureaucracy about the honest and sincere intentions of their new leader has not eroded. While questions about capacity and capability hound most of the federal cabinet's ministers, such critique loses bite when it comes to Khan. Nothing seems to stick. No U-turn makes a difference. No misstep matters. He is Mr Teflon.

In the corridors of power and the anterooms of government offices, a strong belief persists that Prime Minister Khan is at least working hard.

His intentions trump every other failure or shortcoming.

Khan has always been a tireless and selfless campaigner. It is an envious image, developed and cemented over time. Whether it was the cancer hospital, the university, or even politics, Khan was never about himself. He himself boasts that Allah had already given him everything—fame, wealth and global stardom—before he ventured into politics. The foray into the knavish world of politics was not personal but for a national cause.

Khan's supporters say his drive and energy are unparalleled. It is in stark contrast to many of his predecessors, who lapped up the comforts of the office and slacked in luxury.

'You can see that he is putting in an effort,' said a senior military official who spoke on condition of anonymity as he is not authorized to talk to the media. 'The government has made a good start. It has taken steps in the right direction.' The men in uniform invariably seem to share this sentiment, no matter whether they are posted in the GHQ or outback in the country.

Many civilians feel the same way.

'I have worked with several governments. However, this time it is different. The intentions of those at the top are honest and sincere,' said Sakib Sherani, who is advising the government on the economy.

A bureaucrat, who also spoke on condition of anonymity, echoed the sentiment.

'I also have great admiration for Imran Khan because his belief system is radically different from the decadent ideological worldview that both Nawaz Sharif and Asif Ali Zardari had,' the bureaucrat said.

The regard and goodwill that Khan enjoys, said the official, is 'primarily because of the nature of his political struggle, his honesty of convictions, and his humility and compassion despite the tsunami of political appeal that he enjoys as a leader'.

Khan's untainted image, unblemished by charges of corruption and financial wrongdoing, has eclipsed every personal failing and episode of political naiveté.

'Imran Khan is not financially corrupt,' said Sheraz Malik, a Lahore-based economics teacher and a supporter of PTI. 'And he genuinely wants Pakistan to succeed. You can see it in his words and actions that he deeply cares about fixing Pakistan.'

Khan's supporters feel that sincerity in his high baritone voice, even in his grimaces and facial contortions during public speeches, and in his deliberately unfussy sartorial choices.

'He has enduring goodwill because his goodwill has endured,' Malik said. 'We're a land of fallen heroes. Whoever we make a hero turns out to be just a scam. They develop goodwill, but they do not live up to it; their goodwill fades,' he added.

'Imran Khan has stood up and kept standing even when you laughed at his dharnas, at his civil disobedience, at his childish push-ups for breakfast.'

Khan often shoots from the hip. Several of the gaffes and faux pas of the current government and Khan would have damaged anyone else irreparably. But Khan has managed to shrug off any such embarrassments. To his supporters, he is a lovable novice at a game where the other players are cynical old hands.

At the ceremony marking the government's 100 days in office, Khan's reference to chickens and eggs, buffaloes and cows elicited loud cackles from his opposition. During the speech, when he said that the government 'would give eggs', there was loud laughter from those present. As the camera panned to the audience, several female supporters could be seen laughing and clapping, but 'It's okay. Khan is a simple man,' one in attendance put it later.

Many of his critical statements would be anathema to anyone else's political career. When he criticized the military, he was a no-holds-barred critic. But that did not stop Khan from coming to the forefront of national politics.

In a recent interview with a panel of talk show hosts, Khan said the military stands behind his party's manifesto. Any other politician in the past would have been reprimanded by the military and reminded that it does not stand behind any political party's manifesto. But this time, the military spokesperson explained untroubled: the prime minister's statement was made in a specific context.

Critics say that the dragnet of accountability has been thrown around leading politicians in a bid to weed out the old political elite and ensure that Imran Khan faces no opposition.

Admirers of Khan vehemently deny these assertions. And insist with conviction that the day is not far when NAB turns its attention to Khan's own party and that Khan will not lift one finger to help anyone hide ill-gotten wealth. Convinced quarters hint that the day is not far when these convictions will be duly tested, and Khan will prove himself without hesitation.

Some contend that Khan gets away with his political U-turns because he has been a national icon and celebrity for decades, idolized by both women and men.

'Imran is a post-colonial sports icon whose sexualized masculinity matches only that of a film star, and hence hypnotic adulation follows him,' said R.A. Siddiqui, a professor of politics and international relations. 'This image overrides his political fumbles. Pakistan has had a love affair with Imran Khan for a very long time. Even at sixty-six, he is like an old flame. Like all love affairs, it is irrational.'

Khan's supporters take exception to this view and say that corruption is a far more significant and pervasive problem for people than most analysts like to admit. They stress that Khan's support persists because he represents the anti-corruption and anti-status quo.

'Underneath it all, we do not care whom he marries, if he eats "kukkar" or "katta", if he prays or preys. If his following was for his personality, then people will clearly be disturbed by this kind of demeanour,' Malik said. 'It's standing up to a rigged system, which we, the people, have to put up with every day, that makes us stand behind him.'

It is too early to tell whether this goodwill and popularity will last throughout the full term. But Khan enjoys a unique position, unfettered by the circumstances and compulsions of past prime ministers, and buttressed by a deep well of goodwill, almost cult-like adulation, among his supporters.

Only Khan can fail himself now.

Chapter 26

A Presidential System Down the Horizon

January 2019

Pakistan's experience with parliamentary democracy has not been very enviable. Political parties have failed to make the most of this system. Each experience of democratic tenure has resulted in sheer disappointment if not failure. In the early and mid-1990s, corruption tainted the two major political parties. After the Musharraf years, the transition to parliamentary democracy has again been overshadowed by allegations of corruption and plundering of public funds on an unprecedented scale. A debate is expected to start in the country soon about the viability of the parliamentary system and whether Pakistan would be better off with the presidential system.

The real power brokers have been grappling with this idea for quite some time, and there is a strong sentiment in favour of a presidential system. There are two models of the presidential system in review: the American system or the semi-presidential system of France. In the latter order, the president appoints a prime minister but retains control over the real levers of power. The Turkish model is also of particular interest. The major ruling parties would be averse to a presidential system of governance. However, Khan might relish it. And the PTI government might end up doing the legwork for an eventual change of system in the country.

Already, some columns have appeared in the Urdu press, stressing the need to have a presidential system and diluting on the failures of parliamentary democracy. Interestingly, some astrologers and tarot card readers that TV shows hosted in the last week of 2018 also predicted a presidential system for the country. It appeared more like a public opinion-moulding campaign than a genuine gaze into the crystal ball.

Nonetheless, if one attempts to give a political prognosis without relying on the cosmic tabulation, the following are the contours of the emerging scenario in the medium-long term: the Arab countries will bankroll the current government away from default after agreements have been sealed with the backing of the Establishment. Relations with China will be drastically recalibrated, and many of the pacts and projects signed by the previous government will either be revised or shelved. The lessons learned from the years of engagement with the US have made the (deep) state wary of getting entangled in a similar arrangement with another power. Internally, all the notables of the political class who defined the politics of the last two decades will be made to fade away ingloriously. The Establishment has spurned dynasty politics. The media is already tamed and cowed down; further restrictions will be imposed on social media. A Chinese model of the Internet seems very appealing to the powers that be.

A dominant player of the Establishment once hailed Khan as the only honest politician. Most of the commandments of that player have come true: the judiciary coming in to check the errant politicians and governments, mainstreaming religious militants into politics and marginalizing the entrenched politicians and their progeny. The last unfinished business is the introduction of the presidential system.

Gradually but surely, a new system led by a strong man—once the dawn of Imran Khan-led change fades away—beckons us.

Chapter 27

Prime Minister Khan's Angry Moment

Critics say the prime minister is too focused
on the rear-view mirror and not looking
at the dangers ahead

26 April 2019

Prime Minister Khan is angry. He fired broadsides at his political opponents during a rally in South Waziristan in a sign that he will not be cowed down as criticism of his style of governance and the lacklustre performance of the federal government mounts. In a raucous speech, the prime minister even threw some salvos that were politically incorrect and misogynistic. The prime minister insists that he will not relent in pursuing corruption charges against the leadership of the two main opposition parties. The fight against corruption is the raison d'être of his politics.

In his speech, Prime Minister Khan reiterated that the corruption of past rulers was the primary cause of the current economic whirlpool. 'When the money is laundered abroad, it creates shortages of the dollar and leads to a devaluation of local currency and inflation, which hits the common man,' he said. It is simplistic and, some would argue, a half-baked diagnosis of the economic ailment. But it was this simplicity of message and sincerity of intentions that, among some other factors, catapulted Imran Khan to become the prime minister. He remains on point. But critics say the prime minister is too focused on the rear-view mirror and not looking at the dangers ahead.

The sacking of Asad Umar, the former finance minister, and the shuffling of a couple of other cabinet ministers gravely dented the party's image. The idealism and optimism of the pre-election campaign have dissipated. The bubble has burst. Even staunch supporters of PTI are left red-faced, finding it difficult to defend the latest turn of events and repeated 'slips of the tongue'. The constant bashing of past governments has not helped to neutralize the rising discontent on the streets.

The shuffling of the deck in the federal cabinet has given the prime minister a breather. However, it is a temporary relief. Some cabinet ministers are already saying that they will be back in their previous positions within a few months. The internal party differences, conspiracies and sniping are emasculating the government's ability to perform. The ineptitude of the core team of the ruling party has come as a rude awakening.

The enormous economic challenges will hamper the prime minister's reform and social welfare agenda and further fuel disgruntlement. Hafeez Sheikh, the new finance minister, has his work cut out as he attempts to turn around the economy when all indicators are showing a negative trend in the near future.

Meanwhile, backstage manoeuvring and wheeling-and-dealing have started. In the first stage, Punjab is the focus of such intrigue. The chief minister, Usman Buzdar, is struggling to counter a barrage of criticism about his competence and ability. Calls for his ouster are gaining increased resonance. Punjab Governor Chaudhry Muhammad Sarwar is also finding himself on slippery ground. It remains to be seen who comes out unscathed from the current political tumult that is brewing in Punjab. Powerful lobbies and power brokers inside and outside of politics are at play. Prime Minister Khan will have to take decisions about Punjab soon. The status quo is untenable; some changes are inevitable. Lingering over the tough decision would cause further complications.

The opposition is gearing up for street agitation by June; the political temperature is bound to rise in the summer. However, the opposition, barring a few religious figures, lacks the wherewithal to mount a sustained campaign of street protests. The new interior minister, Brigadier Ijaz Shah (retd), has already cracked the whip and hinted at dealing with the opposition with brute force.

Amid all this political uncertainty and instability, the peculiar speculation about the need for a presidential system of government has found further currency. The powerful security establishment is not averse to the idea; several top officials have been found praising the presidential system in private and semi-official settings. Supporters of Prime Minister Khan also see their salvation in the presidential order, where he is free from the push and pull of allied political parties and the incompetence of his party members.

The parliament has been reduced to an arena filled with raucous. It echoes inane and obscene potshots at political opponents and remains unable to carry out necessary legislation. There is a need to develop a political consensus. For now, neither side is willing to sit down and initiate a political dialogue.

Prime Minister Khan feels such dialogue is unnecessary. It is tantamount to giving legitimacy to those he has branded and condemned as corrupt. His public posture is increasingly aggressive and confrontational. He wants to crush the opposition entirely and totally. Also, he is frustrated with his team. No wonder he sounds angry.

The government's detractors view the rising set of challenges and the continuous fumbling and faltering of the government as a gradual and slow retreat into a political dead end. It does not bode well for the democratic setup—a political logjam risks bringing the whole house down.

Chapter 28

Shambolic Governance and
Economic Meltdown

May 2019

It was always about the economy. When Gen. Qamar Javed Bajwa, the army chief, spoke at a seminar about the interplay of the economy and security in Karachi in 2017, he said he was concerned about the country's low tax-to-GDP ratio, the current account imbalance, the lack of tax reforms, the documentation of the economy, diversifying the export base and sustainable growth through savings and investments. Like all past episodes, it was the powerful establishment showing the civilian leadership the way forward, officials said.

However, PTI has made the wrong calculation. Its ministers are continuously harping on an old trope: previous governments are responsible for the current mess. Every day of every week, ministers, state ministers, advisors and special assistants to the prime minister drill this message. We get it. We seriously get it. However, that is precisely why the voters brought Khan to power—to fix the emaciated, stubborn, debt-ridden economy.

Nine months into power, the government is flailing and failing. Asad Umar was always inexplicably laughing and giggling, trying to assure the compatriots as he attempted his out-of-the-box approach. His junior, Hammad Azhar, also tries to give similar assurances with a sombre and serious face. Hammad offloads a tonne of statistics, figures and verbal charts of past performance, but an ordinary person sees the bottom line. The bottom line is simple: is he better off or worse off?

The original economic duo could satisfy neither the business community nor the people. Asad was shafted and his replacement, Abdul Hafeez Shaikh, is equally struggling to ease the jitters and unease.

The perception that the new economic team has been installed at the behest of foreign lenders has dented the political government's credibility.

The last few days have been telling and alarming. The rupee has seen depreciation like never before. The US dollar is skyrocketing. The country's debt and liabilities have gone up by $10.6 billion in the first nine months of the ongoing fiscal year. Exports have failed to pick up; they were reduced by 1.54 per cent to $2.09 billion in April this year. The foreign exchange reserves remain under pressure. The International Monetary Fund's $6 billion bailout package was supposed to bring some stability to the economy. However, there is panic everywhere.

The economy is choking. The informal economy, which has always provided a cushion, is also halting because of the accountability drive. There is no major spending by the government; it has no money. Businesspeople are not making payments. As a result, receivables have shot up; there is no liquidity in the system. The wheel has stopped turning.

Meanwhile, the spectre of terror has raised its ugly head. Balochistan has been reeling from a new wave of terror as Gwadar and its adjoining areas have come under renewed terrorist attacks. It is a signal that CPEC will remain a target. Lahore saw terror bombing after a long gap. The Islamic State has conspicuously announced its presence in the country. It is a foreboding sign.

For any government, it is a deeply troubling scenario.

But Prime Minister Khan and his team—both the original and borrowed one—seem unconcerned by the buildup of public disquiet and discomfort. The prime minister has been persistently telling people not to worry. His exhortation, '*Aap nai ghabrana nahin* [You do not have to panic],' is failing to calm the nerves.

On several occasions, the prime minister has asked the people to pray. Pray for the economy. Pray for offshore oil and gas exploration. His ministers have been making desperate and hollow claims.

Some weeks ago, Faisal Vawda, a minister in Khan's cabinet, said that within days there would be a rain of jobs and economic opportunities. That deadline passed without a whimper of embarrassment. The straight-faced hollow promises and the angry-faced fulminations to drag the opposition politicians over the coals of accountability seem comical ploys to distract from government hobbling.

The message conveyed to the world during foreign visits about rampant corruption back home has boomeranged. Investor confidence has been low. Just as an example, meetings after meetings have been conducted in the Prime Minister's Office since last year to work on fintech. However, what is the result? There is no immediate good news. PayPal has declined to come to Pakistan. The big industry is also showing reluctance. The French giant Renault has also apparently put its plans for investment on hold.

People want to know what the economic roadmap is. The country is hurtling towards stagflation. How will the government cover for the ordinary folks? The communication strategy of the government has been off-key.

For every government step, every move and every policy measure, there is readily available a blistering and contradictory statement by Prime Minister Khan from his opposition days. WhatsApp groups are rife with such videos and memes. Never have past words and statements come back to haunt a government like the current one.

The urban-educated middle-class PTI base is not blindly following the party anymore. It is questioning the party and, more so, questioning their own judgement.

The opposition has failed to capitalize so far because the principal leadership has been ensnared in court cases. Asif Ali Zardari is trying to dodge another jail term while Nawaz Sharif is back in prison. Shehbaz Sharif is looking for ways to escape.

But a perfect storm is building up. The rumblings and disgruntlement on the street, the pain experienced by consumers, especially the middle-class, and the anxiety and apprehensions of the business community are all ideal ingredients for a big crisis to suddenly erupt and snowball. The latest development of the Bilawal Bhutto-Zardari and Maryam Nawaz Sharif meeting will add a new zest to the opposition's morale.

During his 2017 speech in Karachi, Gen. Qamar Javed Bajwa said that he reads the business section of the newspaper after looking at the front pages. These days, they must make for an uncomfortable read.

Chapter 29

Gen. Bajwa Gets a One-Term Extension

20 August 2019

Prime Minister Khan on Monday announced a three-year extension to the term of Army Chief Gen. Qamar Javed Bajwa, who was earlier scheduled to retire in November this year.

The extension means Gen. Bajwa, a powerful army chief under whose tenure the influence of the military has increased tremendously in the country, would lead the army till the end of 2022.

The 'decision was taken in view of the regional security environment', was a brief statement from the Prime Minister's Office. It was seen as a reference to the escalating tensions with India over the disputed Kashmir region and neighbouring Afghanistan, where negotiations are underway between the Taliban and the United States; Pakistan is expected to help seal the deal.

The extension was widely expected, as speculation had been rife for months that the powerful military chief would stay on. Such speculations often start swirling whenever an army chief nears retirement. Gen. Bajwa's predecessor retired on time, but the term of another former army chief, Gen. Ashfaq Parvez Kayani, was extended in 2010.

The army chief is the country's most powerful position, and the military has traditionally overshadowed the civilian governments, which have remained mired in allegations of corruption and incompetence. But Prime Minister Khan, who came to power last year, and Gen. Bajwa have worked in tandem; their harmony and teamwork over domestic and security policies have been a stark contrast to previous civilian leaders and army chiefs, who were often at loggerheads over policy issues.

Analysts said the decision by Khan to give an extension to Gen. Bajwa will naturally have far-reaching impacts.

Gen. Bajwa is expected to play a pivotal role in delivering on Afghanistan as the Taliban and the United States come closer to ending the years of war. He has been very vocal in stressing that armed militant groups have no space inside Pakistan. Such groups are more of a liability than an asset in the changing international environment and would be dealt with a stern hand.

On the Indian front, Gen. Bajwa will have to confront an ever-aggressive and, in Pakistan's view, expansionist Modi regime that has shown no appetite for dialogue to resolve the outstanding issues between the two nuclear-armed neighbours. Under Gen. Bajwa's command, India blinkered after the Pulwama military blows. The nation expects Gen. Bajwa to ensure that Indian designs towards Pakistan remain a pipe dream and the country maintains its dignity, territorial integrity and standing. It may be noted that India has consistently maintained that it has not violated an international border and has denied the Pakistani assertions of the same.[*]

---

[*] Tribune, 'India a Rogue State: Moeed Yusuf, *Express Tribune*, 18 May 2021, https://tribune.com.pk/story/2281096/india-a-rogue-state-moeed-yusuf.https://tribune.com.pk/story/2281096/india-a-rogue-state-moeed-yusuf, accessed on 21 March 2024.

Some critics viewed the extension given to Gen. Bajwa as Khan trying to ensure his own political survival. In the past, Khan had been critical of extensions given to army and intelligence chiefs, stressing that such moves weakened the institution.

Gen. Bajwa portrayed himself as a staunch believer in civilian supremacy when he was appointed by former prime minister Nawaz Sharif in 2016. But the relationship soured soon thereafter. Gen. Bajwa has also built his image as somebody who is uncompromising against corruption, which fits in with Prime Minister Khan's anti-corruption campaign.

Khan has pressed hard to go after opposition politicians, accusing them of corrupt practices and amassing enormous wealth while in office. Several top politicians, including former prime ministers Nawaz Sharif and Shahid Khaqan Abbasi and former president Asif Ali Zardari, are currently in jail over corruption allegations. Opposition politicians have accused Khan of political victimization.

Gen. Bajwa is expected to continue providing support to Khan's political government, which faces the enormous challenge of revitalizing the country's anaemic economy.

Officials of Khan's political party, PTI, welcomed the news in almost celebratory tones. 'I welcome the extension of Gen. Bajwa's term for another term. His leadership, integrity, and patriotism are critical at this crucial juncture when Pakistan is facing a grave crisis in Kashmir,' Naeemul Haq, a close aide to Khan, stated in a message on Twitter. 'The whole nation can feel comfortable that the leadership of our armed forces is in good hands.'

Chapter 30

Maulana Fazal-ur-Rehman's Game Plan

8 November 2019

For years, Maulana Fazal-ur-Rehman lived with the reputation of being just another political wheeler-dealer. In successive governments, he managed to extract substantial gains through deft and pragmatic negotiating and bargaining skills.

It changed after the setback in the 2018 General Elections when he found himself off the playing field. From day one, Maulana has cried foul and blamed the Establishment for denying him and the rest of the current opposition political parties a level playing field. He was seething in a press conference soon after the elections and urged the rest of the opposition not to accept the results. He also called for mass resignations. But the exhortations went in vain, as other opposition politicians opposed the move.

More than a year later, Maulana has flipped the political game on its head. He has replicated the past protest campaigns of PTI and Tahir-ul Qadri. Maulana's protest campaign is political and personal. The constant mockery that Prime Minister Imran Khan heaps on him irritates him. It has become a rivalry that is both bitter and irreconcilable.

With thousands of supporters, Maulana is staying put in the federal capital. By managing to draw a sizeable crowd as it meandered through several big cities of the country and galvanized the anti-government sentiment, Maulana has raised his political stature. He is now someone who can rattle the cage. He has also forced the other two opposition political parties to stand by him, if not behind him, as he spearheads the first significant political challenge to the government of Prime Minister Imran Khan.

The PTI government has begun the negotiation process despite initially spurning such a possibility. The government was forced onto the back foot from the get-go. It was compelled to allow easy entry for the protesters into the capital. The restrictions on mainstream media have failed to dent the protest as social media continues to provide an alternative and more widespread space.

The decision not to go towards the Red Zone has been a masterstroke. The government cannot use force to disperse the existing crowd, which has remained peaceful and shown no signs of embarking on a violent confrontation with the law-enforcing authorities. But the initiative rests with Maulana. Whenever he feels cornered or conned in the ongoing negotiations, he can raise the stakes and order his supporters to start the march towards the sensitive government locations. Maulana has also recovered from the setbacks of the PPP and PML–N, staying away from his prolonged sit-in plan.

One of the spin-offs of the current political turbulence has been the apparent relaxation of the PML–N leadership. Nawaz Sharif and Maryam Nawaz Sharif are both out of prison and ensconced in Jati Umra. There is an expectation that Asif Ali Zardari will also soon find himself in a hospital bed in the custody of NAB.

Maulana has used political rhetoric in a clever and calibrated manner. His statements forced the ISPR to initially issue a stern counterstatement. But ISPR mellowed its posture on Wednesday, reiterating that the army has nothing to do with politics. Part of it is due to the backchannel talks. The Chaudhrys of Gujrat, the oracles of political mediation and bargaining, have been employed to find a middle ground.

Being a political animal who has been part of the rough and tumble of Pakistani politics for decades and is strongly familiar with the ways the Establishment plays its game, Maulana must have calculated his game plan long ago. One does not expect the wily religious politician to gamble everything on a zero-sum game.

Chapter 31

The Penitence of PML–N

Some have termed it a capitulation.
Some have called it pragmatism

28 April 2020

The PML–N is going through a transmogrification. The party leadership has realized that it overplayed its hand when it tried to thumb its nose at the circles of power. Its pre-election slogan, 'Give Respect to the Vote', now seems like a painful reminder of a political misstep. In private conversations, leaders concede that the decision to try to take on the state institutions was a fatal mistake. The headiness of the pre-election slogans, the passion, and the energy of the narrative are punctured. It all seems like a nightmare that could have been avoided. There is a wringing of hands. There is lingering regret.

But let me digress for a bit.

Yusuf Raza Gilani, the former PPP prime minister, has shared a wonderful anecdote about politics. Gilani narrates how once, in the late 1980s, he was told by his uncle, Pir Pagara, to start lobbying to be the Punjab chief minister. At that point, Nawaz Sharif was the chief minister of the province and had tried to assert his independence. Gilani, who was the railways minister at the time, started a campaign in all earnestness. After some time, when Gilani thought he had mustered the support of enough members of Parliament, he went back to his uncle with the news. The uncle laughed him off and revealed that he had just used the young nephew for a bigger political ploy. 'We just wanted to teach Nawaz Sharif a lesson,' the elder Pagara said. Gilani says he felt bitter about it since he had been on very good terms with Nawaz Sharif before that episode.

The story shines a light on the real game of politics. People are expedient, and so are the ideals. At the altar of politics, principles are the first casualty. And the biggest rule of the game in Pakistani politics is that there are no rules.

Shehbaz Sharif expressed this frustration in a recent interview with Sohail Warraich. Shehbaz Sharif discloses for the first time that he was holding talks with powerful circles until a month before the elections. The talks deliberated on the future cabinet, he said. Shehbaz Sharif is also not new to the game, and he presumes that similar talks were being held with PTI as well. At the time of the negotiations, Shehbaz Sharif, like any other civilian politician, would have had no way to ascertain the genuineness of the interlocutors on the other side. In fact, the team of interlocutors could have been negotiating in good faith as well. The real intention, the real game plan, would be known only to those at the top of the power pyramid.

And it is also true that just a few weeks before the elections, most political pundits and observers thought that the PML–N would win as it maintained its stronghold over Punjab. This view was shared by many western diplomats and even one official—currently enjoying a senior position in the current set-up—who was an independent observer before the elections.

Shehbaz Sharif now says that the narrative adopted by the PML–N made it lose the election. This realization was present within a group within the party even during the election campaign. While some leaders rallied around Maryam Nawaz Sharif, believing in her message, others reluctantly joined the chorus. They raised the slogans, but their hearts were not in it. They feel that Mian Nawaz Sharif overestimated his popularity and underestimated the extent to which the election campaign could fail.

This grim realization has forced party stalwarts to change their narrative. Since last autumn, the PML–N leadership has started singing a different tune. The absolute cooperation lent to the legislation that gave the army chief another term reflects this realization.

Most of the leadership in the PML–N felt that by extending an olive branch, it could revive its sagging fortunes. Some have termed it a capitulation. Some have called it pragmatism. Some say it is penitence for their gross miscalculation.

But it might be too late. Despite all the speculation about the differences between Prime Minister Khan and the military leadership, there are no signs that a secretive machination is afoot to form a national government in the next few months. In fact, Prime Minister Khan is in a unique position. Despite the bungling of his government over key economic and development issues and the often confused and mixed signals over important policy matters, he is not seen as the problem. The occasional differences do not necessarily indicate a breaking point.

Tariq Aziz, the famous television host who himself dabbled in politics in an unsuccessful attempt, gave a poignant reply once when he was asked about politics. With a deep sigh, Aziz said, 'Politics is heartless.'

By giving conciliatory messages, the PML–N leaders have made yet another gamble, burdened under the weight of their penitence. They are hoping that there will be a soft corner for them in the hearts of the powers that be, which can pave the way for their return to the top.

Chapter 32

Fawad Chaudhry's Gamble

June 2020

Fawad Chaudhry, a key member of Khan's cabinet, has an easy-going charm and sharp wit. His candour is on display in interviews, and he often whips up a storm himself. Having hosted and participated in talk shows over the past several years, he has learned the art of producing a punchy soundbite without much effort. These traits were visible in his latest interview with the Voice of America. In a calm and calculated manner, Fawad Chaudhry laid bare the internal turmoil of the ruling political party. He incisively described how the grouping and infighting within the party have crippled the government.

Fawad Chaudhry heaped the blame on technocrats and unelected advisors who now surround Khan. These elements managed to increase their sway not because of their ability or intelligence, he asserts. They merely filled the chastening power struggles between Jahangir Khan Tareen, Shah Mahmood Qureshi and Asad Umar. Once these political bigwigs entangled themselves in a continuous turf war, the outsiders found a way in.

The minister for science and technology did not accuse the unelected cabinet members of corruption and malfeasance. He simply stated that the unelected coterie of the prime minister has no stake in the game. These outsiders do not share Khan's passion, the urgency of his vision, the ticking clock or the depleting public credibility. All the caveats of having a team without skin in the game have dented Khan's government's popularity and haemorrhaged its functioning. Fawad Chaudhry stated this uncomfortable truth in a simple, matter-of-fact manner. In many ways, his interview was a masterstroke in political messaging.

And he seems to have gotten away with these verbal punches, just like the physical punches he threw at two of his TV critics. During the subsequent cabinet meeting, Prime Minister Khan did not rake Fawad Chaudhry over the coals. Asad Umar's complaint about Fawad Chaudhry's interview did not elicit Khan's ire.

One explanation could be that Fawad Chaudhry's interview was premeditated. Was it a mere coincidence that it was aired just before a weekly cabinet meeting? Some say Prime Minister Khan is acutely aware of the cacophony of criticism surrounding his unelected cabinet members. Fawad Chaudhry, therefore, was used to convey a message to the cabinet. And it has perfect deniability. Fawad Chaudhry has not been part of the inner sanctum ever since he was removed as the information minister.

The other explanation is that Fawad Chaudhry has played solo and gauged the political temperature. He recently tried to convince the prime minister not to embark on a collision course with the judiciary and take back the case against Justice Faez Isa. But his counsel fell on flat ears. So, he does not mind if his political interview, which is fair in its portrayal of the shortcomings and handicaps of the ruling party, ruffles some feathers.

Unlike some other novice colleagues, who are mesmerized by the 'killer smile' and charismatic gait of their leader, Fawad knows that being an 'electable', he does not have to act in an ingratiating manner. He has ample political experience, from the Musharraf days to the government of the Pakistan People's Party. In fact, he is so confident in his ability and intelligence that he felt he was the right choice to be the Punjab chief minister. And, most significantly, he has a good relationship with the most powerful figure in the country. Such proximity and access always result in an increased sense of place and self-worth.

However, Fawad Chaudhry's ambitions are less of a story compared with the tales of ill-governance and incompetence that have tainted the current government. The carefully crafted image of Khan as the saviour against corruption and the status quo is crumbling. The emotion on the street is anger and frustration. Two years after the election, people are now questioning their choice of fervently supporting PTI.

Prime Minister Khan seems to have sensed this lurking storm. That is why he says he is taking things into his own hands: he will personally supervise all aspects of the government; he will personally look after the donation funds; he will personally spearhead the fight against coronavirus; he will personally monitor the violations of the SOPs, etc.

It is really one man against the machine.

But the singular focus on accountability, which critics and observers increasingly see as one-sided and vindictive, and the insistence on refusing a political dialogue with the opposition are further jamming up the machine. The refusal to initiate a political dialogue with the opposition seems like recalcitrance, especially when the 'powers that be' are in contact with opposition figures, making courtesy calls and sounding conciliatory.

It is during such times of political logjam that sharp politicians like Fawad Chaudhry do not shy from taking a contrarian line and gambling for a stake in the future.

This episode should be a moment of worry and reflection for Prime Minister Khan. His base is getting disillusioned. The party leadership is ideologically divided and jockeying for power.

The cabinet is rife with internal discord. At a time when the country faces huge challenges like the COVID-19 pandemic and growing regional tensions, a divisive, shambolic cabinet does not inspire confidence. Prime Minister Khan should create cohesiveness, and the power of the office of the prime minister should not be deferred. A message of unity of command needs to go out to the public.

Otherwise he risks losing control.

Chapter 33

Sharif's Latest Push

22 September 2020

Nawaz Sharif was coy when reporters in London asked him about the plans for the All-Parties Conference. Nawaz Sharif briefly responded that the queries would be answered on the day of the opposition huddle. He was holding the cards close to his chest, but it was also obvious that he was relishing the upcoming occasion.

The Sunday speech was a litany of his old charges. It was a reiteration of 'I will not take dictation' and subsequent face-offs.

This time Nawaz Sharif complained about not having power despite having it three times. He spoke about machinations. Even within the lines, he was shooting barbs.

The speech stunned everyone—even his own party members. It left many party stalwarts nervous about the future. It emboldened the hardliners within the party. Maryam was all aglow. The speech reflected her public pronouncements, mirroring her preferred style of politics. The confrontational tone of the speech is paving the way for her alignment with politics.

But a speech, no matter how bold or divisive, is just words. Political rhetoric needs to be followed by political action.

The real pressure is now on Nawaz Sharif and opposition politicians. Nawaz Sharif has taken an aggressive, extreme position. Will others follow his lead? If they do not, they lose credibility. If they step up, they are taking a position on a defenceless hill, while Nawaz Sharif will simply watch the spectacle from his comfortable apartment in London, unscathed and relatively safe. In the coming weeks and months, the opposition parties have a dual challenge: to stay united and, eventually, to bring out numbers in the streets in December and January. This is not an easy task.

It could well be that Nawaz Sharif's tough posturing is to create just enough political pressure to allow Maryam Chaudhry to leave for London as well. Sharif's newly set up account on Twitter resonates with Maryam's account. Perhaps this is the only reason Sharif has doubled down on his explosive political rhetoric, breaking a long silence. Time will reveal this. After all, Sharif has cut deals in the past.

For Shehbaz Sharif, the implications can be grave. The speech has dented his narrative and the efforts of the past two years to mend fences and effect a rapprochement. His son is already languishing in jail. Are Shehbaz Sharif and some other frontline PML–N leaders ready to pay an even heavier price for Nawaz Sharif's London speech?

Bilawal Bhutto Zardari, the host of the opposition huddle, is gaining invaluable political experience and, with time, can emerge as a key political player. In the current scenario, the PPP will be loath to go all out. It will continue to play both sides.

Maulana Fazal-ur-Rehman, who has the most potent street power, remained in a sulky mood during the opposition moot. His insistence on immediate resignations is not gaining traction with others. Perhaps the biggest hint about what is to come: not much?

But surely there will be heightened political activity, culminating in the March Senate elections.

Prime Minister Khan made a shrewd political move by allowing the speech to be broadcast live. It punctured the criticism of media censorship. But most significantly, the move removed Khan from the direct line of fire. Nawaz Sharif fired salvos that his opponents gleefully portrayed as pushing him further down a dead-end street.

On Monday, further details emerged about a dinner for parliamentary leaders hosted by the top military brass. The military leaders stressed that politicians should themselves settle their political differences and not drag institutions into the muddy waters. Subsequently, questions were raised about the role of politicians who say one thing in public and another in private.

On the face of it, Sunday's development has solidified Prime Minister Khan's political position. Khan has made the calculations. His position is central to the current political calculus. No wonder he chose to spend the weekend in the picturesque Nathia Gali, undisturbed by the commotion of the capital.

Chapter 34

Official Leaks

27 September 2020

Last week, Sheikh Rasheed, the veteran parliamentarian from Rawalpindi, was busy leaking information about meetings of opposition politicians with the military's top brass.* Such disclosures were meant to expose the duplicitous behaviour of opposition politicians, he said.

The timing of the disclosure was key. It came just on the heels of the All-Parties Conference, in which opposition politicians urged free and fair elections without any meddling from outside, demanded the prime minister's resignation, and warned of a protest march towards the capital. But these politicians are two-faced, Sheikh Rasheed said. They meet the powerful figures in private and plead their cases. In public they show a different, defiant face. This will not do, he thundered.

---

* Sheikh Rasheed's 'leaks' were made public during his interactions with local news media and received wide coverage at the time. PTI, 'Pakistan Army, ISI Had Secret Meeting With Opposition Leaders Ahead of Multi-party Conference: Report' *Times of India*, 22 September 2020, https://timesofindia.indiatimes.com/world/pakistan/pakistan-army-isi-had-secret-meeting-with-opposition-leaders-ahead-of-multi-party-conference-report/articleshow/78254114.cms, accessed on 19 March 2024.

These leaks have set off a political scandal. Sheikh Rasheed certainly knows how to work the media. In his recently published autobiography 'From Lal Haveli to the United Nations,' Sheikh writes about his early days in politics and how he used to sit late at night in newspaper offices, ensuring his news was printed. One of his brothers worked briefly as a sub-editor at *Nawa-i-Waqt*, the sister publication of *Nation*. Now, in the age of electronic media, Sheikh Rasheed has kept himself relevant through spicy, witty one-liners and political predictions on television.

While he traded barbs with opposition politicians over their secretive meetings with the top brass, Sheikh Rasheed himself takes pride in such associations. He has mastered the art of speaking with a forked tongue. He likes to throw names at powerful figures in uniform, claiming close bonds and often suggesting that he is speaking on their behalf. It is a perception that Sheikh has built and propagated over his long years in politics. 'Gate No. 4' of the General Headquarters figures repeatedly in his speeches and television appearances. If he could have his way, he would say that he holds the key to the venerated entrance.

Sheikh Rasheed's first encounter, in his own words, with a spy chief was with Lt Gen. Akhtar Abdur Rehman in the early 1980s. He says he impressed the spy chief in the first meeting, which was arranged through an acquaintance, Col. Trimzi. Sheikh used to be summoned by the late general for a meeting every two to three months. 'He used to call me the Rommel of politics,' Sheikh Rashid writes on page 104 of his autobiography. (Erwin Rommel was one of Adolf Hitler's celebrated generals. A military theorist, he was known as the 'desert fox'.)

The remaining part of the autobiography is silent on his subsequent meetings with other intelligence chiefs. Surely there must have been other interactions. I wish Sheikh Rasheed had shed some light on these. Interestingly, on some occasions, Sheikh Rasheed is critical of the political ambitions of two former chiefs, Gen. Aslam Beg and Gen. Asif Nawaz Janjua. With Gen. Musharraf, however, Sheikh struck a close friendship. Gen. Musharraf endearingly called him 'Sheikho'. They often played badminton together and shared a love of Cuban cigars.

Sheikh Rasheed claims he also knows Chief of Army Staff Gen. Qamar Javed Bajwa very well, especially because the chief also studied at Gordon College, Rawalpindi, the alma mater of the veteran politician. It is a curious claim, given the age difference between the two—Sheikh Rasheed being much senior to the army chief. But the army chief is certainly kind to him. Sheikh Rasheed himself acknowledges that his life was saved earlier this year from COVID-19 because he was admitted to the military hospital on the orders of Gen. Bajwa.

This reminds me of what Sheikh Rasheed told me once when I interviewed him during the Panama court case hearings in 2017. He said, 'Remember, friendship or enmity should be just with the "number one".'

Sheikh Rasheed's leaks put PML–N on the back foot. The interview by Director-General ISPR Maj. Gen. Babar Iftikhar further put pressure on the PML–N. The party supporters thought the base was energized after the London speech by Nawaz Sharif. But disclosures that Khawaja Asif had no qualms about seeking the army chief's help on the night of the 2018 elections and Muhammad Zubair's meetings with the army chief pleading the case of both Nawaz and Maryam dented the party's narrative.

However, such backroom meetings and interactions are an essential staple of politics. Not all political conversations take place in the glare of the public spotlight. Such meetings have taken place in the past. They will continue in the future. It is only embarrassing when they become public.

Chapter 35

Imran Meets Trump

July 2019

Fireworks were already expected from the meeting between Prime Minister Khan and US President Donald Trump. But the meeting at the White House exceeded all expectations. The outcome of the meeting enlivened Pakistan and dampened the spirits of the Indians. Khan not only pulled one of the biggest Pakistani crowds in Washington, D.C.'s history but also pulled a diplomatic win on a scale that few people were expecting. President Trump's offer to mediate on the Kashmir issue instantly infuriated the Indians and showcased Khan's success in putting the festering conflict once again under the international spotlight.

Both Trump and Imran enjoyed international celebrity status before their political journeys catapulted them to the highest offices. Both have a populist, nationalist appeal. Both have vowed to make their countries great again. And each of them has been critical of the handling of their respective countries by past rulers.

The commonalities do not end here. Both leaders feel that they are subjected to harsher criticism by their media. Still, there is always an element of uncertainty in such high-stakes meetings, and Khan did appear tentative and conscious in the beginning. But gradually, he eased up after the charm offensive by Trump. 'We were blown away,' Khan said a day after the White House meeting. 'When we met President Trump, the straightforward, charming way he treated us was wonderful,' Khan said while giving a speech at the United States Institute of Peace, a prestigious American think tank.

In a way, the US visit has also given Prime Minister Khan yet another 'I told you so' moment. For years, Khan has railed against the use of military force in the Afghan conflict. He has been one of the most vociferous critics of the use of drone attacks in the Pakistani tribal regions by the United States.

On his first trip to Washington, D.C., since assuming office as the prime minister, Khan gloated at the fact that he was one of the first to suggest that the Afghan conflict was intractable and had no military solution, only a political one. 'When I came here in 2009, I told everyone, including Democratic and Republican leaders, that there is no military solution in Afghanistan. This time, everyone gets that. That is why we will have a good relationship with the US; everyone is on the same page,' Khan said.

Khan has found a willing partner in President Trump. The US president, in his own words, wants to 'extricate' America from the Afghan conflict and has been keen to withdraw the American troops before his election for a second term in office. The Pakistani side is wary of the way Americans left the region after the Russian withdrawal in the 1990s and wants to ensure that the country does not plunge into yet another round of civil war. The geopolitical situation and political compulsions have inadvertently brought both Pakistan and the US closer yet again. Trump chewed back on his harsh criticism of Pakistan in 2018 when he cut off military aid. It is time for a fresh start, he said, as Khan nodded in agreement.

'Islamabad was optimistic about the outcome of the Trump–Khan meeting. But this must have exceeded their wildest expectations, said Arif Rafiq, a political analyst who is based in New York and writes on Pakistan-US relations. 'Trump spoke glowingly of the Pakistani leader and nation after attacking the country in tweets and other public statements throughout last year. The U-turn is remarkable given the tortured history of US-Pakistan relations. But it is also typical of Trump. And it might just be what's needed to bring peace to Afghanistan.'

'Trump is a transactional man looking for a deal, and he may be able to strike a win-win bargain with Islamabad. In exchange for a relatively swift, negotiated exit from Afghanistan, Trump is willing to ease pressure on Pakistan and renew the bilateral partnership,' Rafiq said.

The unexpected offer by the American president to mediate on Kashmir stumped the Indians, who immediately branded Trump a liar.

'Symbolically, Trump's explicit offer to mediate between the two countries is a signal of the changing nature of governance and diplomacy in the Age of Trump. Regardless of India's actual appetite for such intercession, Pakistan will be pleased that a US president has made this offer,' said Mosharraf Zaidi, a prominent foreign policy analyst based in Islamabad.

'If nothing else, it opens the door for Delhi to respond by saying it does not need third parties and looks forward to engaging with Pakistan on Kashmir directly. Trump's keenness for a dignified US exit from Afghanistan is at the heart of this momentary breakthrough in Pakistan,' Zaidi said.

'Many watchers of US-India relations are unhappy with President Trump's suggestion of mediation on Kashmir. They uphold the Indian government's insistence that Kashmir must remain a bilateral issue between India and Pakistan and that senior US leaders must not even mention the word Kashmir,' said Asfandyar Mir, a postdoctoral fellow at the Center for International Security and Cooperation at Stanford University. 'President Trump has angered them by not only mentioning Kashmir but also offering to mediate.'

The tumultuous and often strained relationship between Pakistan and the United States appears 'to have bounced back for now', Mir said. 'There are a lot of issues, but there is a sense in parts of the US government that Pakistan can help in Afghanistan without being sanctioned. The US also feels it needs to keep working with Pakistan on counter-terrorism issues,' he said.

But Mir added a caveat. 'In the case of failures in the Afghan peace process, the relationship will come back under stress again.'

Chapter 36

The Countdown Begins

November 2019

The platelets of Nawaz Sharif never dropped to a life-threatening level. It is all an elaborate hoax. The former prime minister is old and unwell—but not on the death bed. Some close relatives and some officials of the shadowy Deep State cobbled up a scheme to allow Nawaz Sharif to leave the country under the pretext of a grave medical emergency. The medical lab handling the medical tests of the former premier was part of this ingenious scheme and tampered with the results. Prime Minister Khan was kept unaware of the 'deal' and therefore decided to throw a spanner in the works by asking for an indemnity bond.

All the above is obviously just one of the several conspiracy theories doing the rounds in the federal and provincial capitals. The political windmill is churning full throttle with all kinds of rumours and predictions of change. In a time of heightened political polarization and vendettas, facts mix seamlessly with fiction. People only believe what aligns with their political beliefs and preferences. Everything else is a lie, a conspiracy and a ruse.

The illness of the former prime minister, Nawaz Sharif, had indeed upended the political landscape. For weeks, it became the single issue over which the country's politics revolved.

When Nawaz Sharif returned to Pakistan last year, along with his daughter Maryam Nawaz Sharif, he left behind a terminally ill Kulsoom Nawaz Sharif. Political opponents mocked the illness of Kulsoom Nawaz Sharif at that time. Her death failed to shake the conscience of her detractors.

A comparable situation was witnessed recently as questions over the intensity and gravity of the health situation of the former prime minister were raised repeatedly. It was an unfortunate turn of events.

Why does political opposition force us to strip ourselves of the basics of humanity, empathy and kindness? Why has Pakistani politics become so vicious and bloodthirsty? These queries demand deep soul-searching by the political class and the electorate, especially the 'educated, urban class'.

The alarming situation forced even the government's allies to spring into action. Chaudhry Pervez Elahi, the former chief minister of Punjab and current speaker of the Punjab assembly, took to the television screens. Elahi and his cousin Chaudhry Shujaat Hussain are experienced political hands. They know which way the political wind blows and the tact of aggressive and defensive posturing in politics. They advised Prime Minister Khan to show flexibility and large-heartedness by allowing Nawaz Sharif to go abroad. No one wants blood on their hands, and the messaging by the Chaudhrys of Gujrat was not just an expression of their brand of politics. The chairman of the Senate also urged the government to allow Nawaz Sharif to leave the country. It is well-known who pats his back. Some construed these developments as a message forwarded by the Establishment.

At first, Prime Minister Khan had agreed to let Nawaz Sharif leave without conditions, but the hawks in his party soon stopped him. The narrative of PTI is even more potent than those who initially formulated it. It is not letting the party officials recalibrate and compromise. In their view, showing flexibility is a weakness. Part of it is due to the heady feeling one gets while in power. Life in the protected and protocol-heavy government residences and offices always skewed perceptions. Political shifts seem insignificant. The coterie of sycophants convinces the powerful that power will last forever, that no wrong step can ever be taken, and that no lapse of judgement can ever happen. The PTI leadership seems to be in the throes of the same affliction.

Prime Minister Khan has always defied scepticism and done the seemingly impossible. Some around him, therefore, advised him to stick to his guns. They felt that PTI could weather any political storm. The insistence on indemnity bonds was a consequence of this thinking, as the hawks wanted to limit the political fallout of the decision to let Nawaz Sharif go.

The well-wishers of the government have spoken: focus on the economy and governance. Move past the political vendettas. The wish to make political opponents rub their noses on the floor is petty and unbecoming of those holding high offices. The country needs stability for economic progress. It cannot afford to continuously experience political instability spasms. The current imbroglio has brought everything to the edge of a cliff. It is time to throw individual egos over the edge.

Most significantly, the current scenario has undercurrents of a different sort. The allies of the party are feeling uncomfortable and restless. The PTI government is erected on a very fragile foundation; its parliamentary majority is not ironclad. Any opportunity can be seized by the allies to increase their share of the pie. But some analysts are foreseeing political troubles far greater than just the greed of political allies. The usual firefighters, like Jahangir Khan Tareen, are conspicuously quiet and absent from the front lines.

In this backdrop, the meeting between Army Chief Gen. Qamar Javed Bajwa and Prime Minister Khan on Friday assumed great significance. Both leaders met publicly after a long gap. Has the army chief put his weight behind the prime minister or expressed reservations with the government's handling of the ongoing crisis? The coming days will answer this curiosity.

On Saturday, the Lahore High Court allowed Nawaz Sharif to leave the country for four weeks to attend to his medical condition. Meanwhile, Khan has taken the weekend off. The ever-turbulent politics are taking a toll on everyone. Khan is no exception.

After the twenty-two-year political struggle to get to the Prime Minister's Office, Khan is fast learning that governance is not a cakewalk. He will try to rejuvenate himself to return to work next week and will immediately be confronted with a whole new set of challenges.

Chapter 37

The Enigma of Usman Buzdar

April 2020

Usman Buzdar is probably the biggest political mystery in recent years. When he was suddenly plucked out of obscurity and catapulted to the powerful position of Punjab chief minister, the move was met with astonishment and bewilderment.

Many wondered whether Prime Minister Khan had made a blunder in anointing a political novice as the head of the province that determines the fortunes of political parties in the country. Buzdar was immediately written off by his critics and detractors —and political pundits have especially relished in giving cut-off dates of his tenure in office. If one were to believe such predictions, Chief Minister Buzdar would have disappeared into the backwaters of South Punjab long ago.

But Usman Buzdar continues to survive the constant barrage of media onslaught and political attacks. His constant ability to come out unscathed after every new round of political crisis continues to confound and amaze. What is even more surprising is that Chief Minister Buzdar has managed to override some objections raised by some quarters in the powerful Establishment also. His unassuming personality and tentative appearance in social settings further compound the mystery. Despite being in the limelight, Usman Buzdar has resisted the temptations of appearing smug or pompous. During press conferences, he continues to wear a shy smile and in interactions with the prime minister at 7-Club Road, he sits with hands folded and a downcast eye.

Prime Minister Khan continues to believe in his choice. The unflinching belief was evident a few days ago when Chief Minister Buzdar met with Khan at the Prime Minister's House in Islamabad. Hours later it was announced that Azam Sulaiman Khan was removed from the post of chief secretary Punjab. The unceremonious exit of Azam Sulaiman Khan took some people by surprise. After all, he had been posted as the all-powerful chief secretary just a few months ago and had been given a freehand. Three chief secretaries had been removed before him in what seems like a bizarre game of musical chairs. But Azam Sulaiman Khan was thought to have the backing of the powers-that-be. Prime Minister Khan had also shown immense confidence in his administrative skills.

After a constant stream of political criticism of mismanagement and dysfunction in Punjab, a powerful chief secretary and inspector general police duo were put in place. The move was thought to be a workable solution to bring Punjab back on track. It was considered a snub to Chief Minister Buzdar as well. The chief secretary made a point to show that he will not tolerate any political interference and would work independently. And, for a while, Buzdar took the backseat. Political sources said earlier this year that the chief minister was 'playing a waiting game and letting things pile on to the chief secretary' as discontent and unease grew within the local political class. The strategy worked. Chief Minister Buzdar survived yet again, and a once-powerful bureaucrat was made to eat humble pie in an exit from the province.

Aides and political sources say that Chief Minister Buzdar is the quintessential politician from South Punjab: all sweet talk and submissive demeanour but a shrewd and clever political operator from within. They point to the group of twenty Punjab lawmakers who suddenly popped up earlier in January and demanded funds and public projects in their constituencies. Insiders say that the lawmakers' group was a Trojan horse of Chief Minister Buzdar.

Chief Minister Buzdar has also used his former association with the PML-Q to his full advantage. He continues to play a bridge between the PTI and PML-Q. The ability to lend a soft ear to PML-Q while managing the internal grumblings of PTI has added to his longevity in the office.

It could well be that Chief Minister Buzdar has been just plain lucky. His aides, however, insist that luck never has a long shelf-life politics, especially in a province like Punjab where vested interest groups are far too many and far too powerful. Some have speculated for long that more than luck it is the spiritual patronage that has protected Chief Minister Buzdar from the rough and tumble of power politics.

The recent COVID-19 crisis has seen Chief Minister Buzdar come out of his shell. He has been active and at the forefront of the media. The visibility and a growing sense of ease have surprised even those critics who were earlier writing long columns about how he was the single biggest mistake of Prime Minister Khan. Buzdar has emerged as a political survivor with the proverbial nine lives.

Imran Khan was primarily responsible for Buzdar's political survival despite huge opposition. However, Buzdar was forced to resign in March 2022, as a vote of no confidence against Imran in parliament gained momentum. In retrospect, Buzdar's tenure as Punjab's chief minister was largely forgettable, with constant allegations of corruption and kickbacks, and caused significant political damage to PTI. It could be regarded as one of Khan's greatest errors in judgement.

Chapter 38

Senate 2021: Countdown Begins

March 2021

The Crisis

The win of Yusuf Raza Gilani against Hafeez Sheikh seemed to have opened a new window of political possibilities. Suddenly, the whole political calculus was about to change. The ruling party was left reeling, and the extreme shock of an unexpected defeat was writ large on the faces of the cabinet ministers. With just one seat lost, the ruling party was left treading on very fragile, slippery ground while the opposition found wind in its sails.

Some prominent political commentators went as far as to predict that talks about a new political dispensation have already begun between Asif Ali Zardari and Nawaz Sharif, and the powerful backers of the current setup were suddenly portrayed as having lost the initiative.

The hopefuls for change contended that the Establishment had remained neutral in the Senate contest, purposely allowing the political players to play as they pleased. They had finally lost patience with the incompetent ways of the ruling party, they said. And Asif Ali Zardari—the wily politician always so adroit at backroom manoeuvrings and deal-making—was able to play the numbers game to perfection in getting Gilani elected to the upper house of the parliament.

There was strong speculation that Gilani did not enter the race without some solid commitments to a subsequent win as Senate chairman. Otherwise why would a former prime minister of the country run for a Senate seat? Furthermore, Punjab was now being seen as the second battlefield where the power equation was to be changed soon. Grumblings about Usman Buzdar are as old as his elevation as the chief minister of the province. Now, they have found a new resonance and urgency.

Even Prime Minister Khan looked stressed when he came to parliament to secure a vote of confidence. The whole exercise of the confidence vote seemed futile, as it was clear that support in the parliament could be pulled with just a nod from the Establishment, and the whole edifice of the current setup could fall like a pack of cards.

Zoom in

Assumptions about the sudden change of political winds and the notion of 'neutrality', however, lacked clarity. It remained unclear what suddenly snapped and caused the alleged rupture at the top echelons. But both opposition politicians and many of the political pundits, nonetheless, seemed convinced of the unravelling of the current setup, starting with the chairman's Senate vote.

It was not to be. At least not for now.

Sadiq Sanjrani pulled yet another victory from the jaws of an imminent defeat to become the chairman of the Senate for a second term. This was despite the fact that he did not have a numerical majority in the upper house. But his victory was on the cards when he was accurately portrayed by Sheikh Rashid Ahmed as a candidate not only of the ruling party but also of the Deep State. The deputy chairman vote saw a further split in the opposition ranks as Afridi bagged even more votes than Sanjrani.

What happens next?

The PPP is now crying foul, accusing the presiding officer of not playing fair. There are slim chances that it would find recourse on the legal front. PML–N has already complained of pressure from powerful quarters. But this is all posturing.

Beyond the optics, one can see that there is a clear split within the opposition, with its leadership at cross-purposes. It was reflected in the voting during Friday's elections. Insiders claim that PML–N stabbed PPP and Jamiat Ulema-e-Islam (JUI–F) in the back and played a double game. Why would it conveniently hand over the political dividends of its struggle to PPP, a beneficiary of the current setup?

PPP does not want fresh elections before the current government's full tenure. PML–N, on the other hand, is looking for elections before 2023, confident that its vote bank has not been obliterated in Punjab despite the repeated attempts by its detractors. It will not support any move to make Chaudhry Pervez Ilahi the chief minister, as it would be politically detrimental. PTI also does not want to see Pervez at the helm in Punjab. The consensus over Buzdar's replacement, therefore, remains messy.

PML–N and JUI–F will make another push for public agitation now, but the timing for such a move is not right. PPP will continue to try to find space within the system without rocking it too much.

The long view

All of this should be good news for Khan and his party. But Friday's victories offer only temporary relief, and time is not on their side. Much of this year will be spent in small political battles, resulting in debilitating attrition and the erosion of political capital. The true impact of this wrangling will reveal itself in the election year. The perceptional damage done by Hafeez Sheikh's defeat is irreversible.

As damage control, the government will try to further tighten the screws on the PML–N and encourage the intra-Sharif family split. Political instability and friction will increase further and be bound to impact an already fragile economy. It would be nothing short of a miracle if the ruling party managed to turn around the economy while it found itself mired in one political crisis after another in the run-up to the next general elections.

Politics in the country often comes full circle, with respective political parties looking towards the powerful quarters as the final arbiters. This time, it would be no different.

Chapter 39

The Celebrity Twitter Civil Servant

May 2021

The verbal clash between Firdous Ashiq Awan, special assistant to the chief minister of Punjab, and an assistant commissioner, a junior but an important bureaucrat in the district administration, in Sialkot this month touched a raw nerve across different sections of the society. Twitter was ablaze soon after the heated exchange between the two officials went viral. Awan gave a public dressing down to the official over the unavailability of fresh foods and vegetables in the market.

Apparently, the assistant commissioner tried to evade responsibility and the lackadaisical attitude made Awan go ballistic. In a loud and obnoxious manner, the de facto Punjab information minister had a no-holds-barred frontal verbal assault on the civil servant who seemed petrified and deeply offended and felt it better to walk away from the situation before any further escalation.

Soon, the battle lines were drawn. The civil servants quickly closed ranks. A representative body of the officers of the Pakistan Administrative Service expressed deep anguish over the public humiliation of one of its young officers. It commended the officer for maintaining her dignity despite an onslaught that would have unnerved many. The Punjab chief secretary issued a statement condemning the attitude of the minister and said he had expressed his reservations to the chief minister.

Awan remained unrepentant and insisted that the bureaucracy is paid from the taxpayers' money to deliver and not just lord over to give lip service while sitting in chilled offices. Supporters of the ruling PTI were initially a bit hesitant to unequivocally criticize the minister's attitude. But they rallied behind the minister as soon as Maryam Nawaz Sharif, the PML–N leader, expressed support for the bureaucrat. The episode took a political turn as people took positions according to their political leanings.

But, most importantly, the response of the public on Twitter was telling. The clash represented the classic tussle between a politician, trying to show concern for the well-being of its voter, and a bureaucrat, affronted by the uncivilized behaviour of the public representatives playing to the gallery. The heated exchange also signified the public unease with the conduct of the bureaucracy. A large majority of the public lashed out at the bureaucracy for its impervious and colonial mindset. People were quick to note that the bureaucrats cannot act as holier than thou or unaccountable.

While many criticized the harsh mannerisms of the minister, there was an outpouring of criticism and strong disapproval of the latest trend among recent graduates of the Civil Services Academy (CSA) to use Twitter and other social media apps for what is widely seen as vain self-projection and glorification. This trend gained momentum under the Khan government, which directed a lot of focus on social media.

Of late, the young bureaucrats have started using social media, especially Twitter, for personal glory. They proudly post pictures while sitting inside or standing next to the expensive government SUVs, surrounded by gun-toting security guards, and yet complain of tough working conditions. They seek praise and self-validation for doing every obligatory and essential aspect of their official jobs, which are paid for by public tax money. Furthermore, they want applause for even the smallest parts of their duties. In one cringe-worthy post, an assistant commissioner boasted that he spent Valentine's Day undercover and visited different markets to inspect commodity prices. But he also had a camera loyally following every move subsequently posted on Twitter.

Many people, including senior retired civil servants, find such exhibitionism in bad taste. Gone are the days when a civil services officer was the embodiment of decency, sophistication, and refinement, they lament. Nowadays, a new lot of assistant commissioners and assistant superintendents, especially, have confused their jobs with existential rants, self-congratulatory posts, and stylised pictures. Dressed in branded clothes, official visits have become mere photo-ops. There is almost a sense of rivalry among these young CSA graduates with sporting stars and showbiz celebrities for public approval and adoration. The civil servants who earlier aspired to be role models for society now seem obsessed with just being models.

This is not to suggest that the use of Twitter and other social media apps should be discarded altogether. Social-media apps have broken the proverbial barrier between the public and civil servants. Access has become easier. A complainant does not have to keep dialling an unresponsive official number to reach an officer. A mere tweet can set off quick redressal of problems, many of which need immediate and urgent action.

But the trend of the young bureaucrats to play to the gallery and constantly seek self-validation needs to be checked. It is problematic if action is taken merely through Twitter complaints while the majority of people, who don't have access to social media or are not as tech-savvy to compile compelling threads about their problems, continue to writhe on the sidelines unheard and unattended. Often it seems that complaints addressed through Twitter are aimed just at gaining popularity and the action is not taken with a sense of duty and official obligation.

The government should formulate guidelines for the use of social media by officials. An official Twitter handle may be maintained for the position, not the person. This should be managed by an official public relations officer (PRO), not the civil officer himself/herself. A personal account should not be linked, nor mentioned. A civil officer may add 'public good' pictures without self-projection. Personal pictures should be strictly censured if posted via official handles. In the case of a municipality head or district head, one account should suffice.

There is a scene in the cult classic movie *American Psycho*, starring Christian Bale. Several characters pull up fancy and yet indistinguishable business cards, each 'Wall Street Yuppie' trying to outdo and impress the other in an almost manic and psychopathic manner. The young officers of the Pakistan Administrative Service and Police Service of Pakistan cadre are acting in a similar manner by posting tweets just to get brownie points and validation from the public.

The public is actually having none of it.

Chapter 40

Gathering Storm

August 2021

The trajectory of Pakistan–US relations has never run smoothly. It is a relationship that has seen constant crests and troughs. Bilateral ties are often described as transactional, with deep-rooted antipathy and mistrust. The last brief period of bonhomie came when former army chief and president Gen. Musharraf joined the 'war against terrorism'. Gen. Musharraf remained an indispensable ally before being spurned as a pariah.

The differences between Pakistan and the US grew wider as the war in Afghanistan dragged on. All signs are that the bilateral relationship is going downhill again. Americans have long complained that Pakistan has not exerted enough pressure on the Taliban to reduce violence inside Afghanistan. The cacophony of complaints is likely to get louder.

In many ways, the essential difference over how to deal with the Afghan conundrum has remained the same. Pakistani Generals feel that their advice was never taken seriously by the Americans. The concern of the Pakistani establishment about the Indian footprint in Afghanistan was shrugged off soon after 9/11. In the subsequent years, the strategic partnership between the US and India only grew stronger and crystallized in terms of greater cooperation, while Pakistan continued to be viewed with suspicion and latent hostility.

Lt Gen. Mahmood Ahmed, the director-general of ISI in 2001, told the Americans, among other things, that the Afghan terrain is such that a foreign military occupation force would always find itself struggling. Gen. Mahmood was subsequently sidelined for being too sympathetic towards the Taliban. Gen. Ashfaq Pervez Kayani had extensive and intensive interactions with US officials during his tenure, as he urged the Americans to focus on stabilising Afghanistan. Within the American establishment, however, competing and, at times, parallel policy priorities and preferences made that goal elusive. The mantra of Pakistan playing a double game, taking US aid from one hand, and feeding the Taliban from the other, remained a constant chorus.

Now, after twenty years, as the US has finally left Afghanistan, many in Pakistan feel validated for being sceptical and wary of the US. The relationship, no matter how glossed over and polished under diplomatic verbiage, has never been stable.

There is a deep resentment within the Pakistani defence and diplomatic communities about the transactional nature of the relationship. But there is also a realization that Pakistan cannot throw punches above its weight. Army Chief Gen. Qamar Javed Bajwa is acutely aware that the country needs political and economic stability. In fact, economic stability has been one of the core themes of Gen. Bajwa's vision for the country's progress and prosperity. To achieve this aim, the country needs internal stability, and officials say that a conscious decision was made under Gen. Bajwa that no militant armed group would be allowed to operate. Within the last few years, Pakistan has moved swiftly to dismantle armed groups.

The Afghan Taliban, however, poses a much more complicated and tricky problem. They have managed to have deep roots in some urban centres; their sympathizers operate legitimate businesses; and many Pakistanis feel a religious affinity. Officials say that the Afghan refugee camps, fortified over the last thirty years, act as sanctuaries where any armed action by the Pakistani forces can have serious security implications. The vast numbers of madrassas spread across the country remain filled with Taliban sympathizers.

The Taliban leadership—with a political base in Doha and military inside Afghanistan—feels it has the upper hand. Buttressed by the tacit support of China, Iran and Russia, the Taliban feel their time has finally arrived. They remain reluctant to share power with the other Afghan groups. Even if they agree to any such formula, their demand is for the lion's share, which is unacceptable to the detractors. Pakistan, officials say, has been trying for a negotiated, all-inclusive political settlement, but Afghan history is marked by a lack of power sharing.

Meanwhile, the Taliban are making rapid advances on the ground. The Kabul regime has concentrated itself in some major cities and plans to check Taliban advances on these fronts. But as the rest of the country falls to the Taliban, the sense of vulnerability among anti-Taliban forces grows exponentially. Pakistani leaders are hedging their bets on their course of action if Kabul eventually falls to the Taliban. It is a bridge that seems distant but is not too far. A long, protracted civil war is becoming more likely.

Pakistani leadership feels it will come under renewed pressure—even sanctions if there is a complete rupture in bilateral relations—from the US as frustration and anger over the Afghan failure of twenty years mount in Washington, D.C. There is also a sense that the Pakistani perspective has not been communicated and projected properly to the outside world. The compulsions, the hard-fought battles against local militants, the tightrope walk—it all has found not much sympathy in most capitals of the world. Pakistan has done all it could to sway the Taliban, and going any further against the Taliban, who are feeling wind under their wings, would lead to a serious blowback. The country simply cannot afford another war inside its borders, officials assert.

Now, there will be another push to amplify Pakistan's messaging as new security threats emerge and geostrategic shifts take place. Strategic communication in the public and diplomatic domains, however, has not proven to be highly effective in the past. The political leadership needs to ponder the reasons for this. Have they spent more time preaching to the converted and less time building capacity, credibility and global acceptability? Why is it that the adversaries managed to achieve their strategic goals while the country remains mired in political strife and economic uncertainty, unable to articulate its position effectively on the global stage?

There are no easy answers to these questions, but work is cut out for the government of Prime Minister Khan.

The times ahead are turbulent, and the challenge is immense. Mere tweeting sprees by federal ministers on foreign policy will not cut any ice.

Chapter 41

The Fall of Kabul

What happens next?

August 2021

In Kabul, Ashraf Ghani's regime spectacularly ended after a fast-moving series of events that shocked and surprised many analysts and commentators. The Taliban took Kabul back seamlessly, without the bloodshed and violence that were commonly expected.

Ghani decided to flee, along with two of his trusted aides, stuffing his entourage of SUVs and a helicopter with money, some of which did not even fit in the helicopter.

Ghani, who latched on to power despite losing the real mandate in the last Afghan elections, lacked credibility and legitimacy; corruption was rife and rendered his regime ineffectual. Without American support, thinking about challenging or confronting the Taliban was a pipe dream. The bravado exhibited by his regime vanished into thin air. The Afghan National Army, despite being armed to the teeth, surrendered ignominiously. But even the Taliban did not expect the speed with which they were able to retake Kabul, a fact acknowledged by Mullah Baradar in a statement.

Questions are now being asked about the failure of American and other intelligence agencies to accurately predict the speed and effectiveness of the Taliban blitzkrieg. 'Nobody expected the way it happened so fast,' a senior Pakistani official in Islamabad said Monday, referring to the Taliban takeover.

Now that the Taliban are back in the saddle, regional powers and their immediate neighbours are assessing the constantly evolving situation.

The big question is: what happens next?

Officials in Islamabad say there are several suggestions to make the Taliban and their detractors agree on a political settlement. But the situation remains fluid.

Pakistan is hosting a delegation of leaders from the former Northern Alliance as discussions about the future setup in Afghanistan gain momentum. The leaders of the former Northern Alliance will go back to talk to the Taliban about a future dispensation. It remains to be seen whether the Taliban will be accommodating to any other group, Pashtun, or non-Pashtun. Pakistan wants a politically inclusive settlement, and officials say all their efforts are geared towards that end. Officials say the country is also reaching out to Iran, as there is a feeling that not keeping Iran in the loop in the past was a mistake.

Officials in Islamabad have also heaved a sigh of relief that there has been no bloodshed or anarchy in the Taliban takeover, although the possibility of violence cannot be ruled out in the future. Pakistani officials do not foresee an immediate refugee crisis either. Those moving towards Pakistan will be stopped at the borders and treated as internally displaced people and not as economic refugees. But it is too early and remains to be seen whether a refugee influx will build up in the coming months.

Pakistani officials are also hoping that there will be no human rights violations in Afghanistan under the Taliban. Otherwise, international pressure and opprobrium can fall back on Pakistan. Officials are also cognizant that the scapegoating of the country can happen once the focus of the Europeans and Americans shifts away from the current hectic and panicked evacuation of their citizens and allies from Afghanistan. Statements by cabinet ministers cheering the Taliban takeover have led to diplomatic embarrassment and ruling party members have been told to exhibit restraint and responsibility.

Another big concern is the spillover effect of militancy. The victory of the Taliban in Afghanistan will inevitably result in the emboldening of the militants in Pakistan. Security officials say that Pakistan is hoping that the Afghan Taliban will put the reins on the Pakistani Taliban. 'The Taliban have promised that they will control the TTP,' a senior official said. 'We want them to do more.'

But did anyone ever like the 'do more' mantra?

Afghan Taliban are unlikely to pay heed to Pakistani official pleas.

Chapter 42

Civil–Military Divide

30 October 2021

Senior government officials in Islamabad called an unusual meeting late at night on 29 October as the possibility of a bloody confrontation between law enforcement officials and Tehreek-e-Labbaik, a far-right extremist Islamist group, supporters looms large. The timing and urgency of the meeting, which included senior security officials and cabinet ministers, suggested the gravity of the situation confronting the country as thousands of Tehreek-e-Labbaik supporters, some of them armed, are charging towards the capital, defying calls to peacefully end the protest and showing little interest in negotiations.

Two important messages were conveyed to a select group of media network owners, talk show hosts and journalists during the classified briefing at the intelligence headquarters in Islamabad. First, the armed groups will not be allowed to challenge the writ of the state. Enough is enough. Second, there is no civil–military divide in the country.

A senior security official told the participants that there was no truth in speculations by certain quarters that the recent protest was orchestrated by any internal intelligence agency.

'This is a lie,' the senior security officer said, candidly opening about rumours that the ongoing protest was meant to either destabilize the political government at the behest of the permanent establishment or to revoke the notification about the top spy agency. 'We hear such theories and laugh them off,' the senior security official said.

The official said the Tehreek-e-Labbaik was using religion and emotionally charged slogans to rouse the public, but their real intent was politics through violence and the subjugation of the state. The Labbaik leadership is not willing to engage in meaningful negotiation and instead wants to impose their demands through the use of force. 'The state cannot allow a situation where a group starts to make demands by constantly grabbing its neck,' the senior official said.

The protest is exacting a high toll. It has paralysed life in several cities and choked supply lines to the country's north; even food supplies meant for Afghanistan via the Torkham border have come to a standstill. Four police officers lost their lives and 114 were wounded, at least ten of them critically, due to the violent clashes.

The official acknowledged that the district and police administrations lacked the wherewithal to control such a large, violent mob and have always failed to stop Labbaik advances in the past. It has been no different this time. But now the situation was fast moving towards a head-on collision as the Punjab Rangers, the paramilitary troops, had taken position and would not allow Labbaik to move past Wazirabad.

Officials say that the Rangers will have no option but to shoot back if someone in the crowd opens fire, contrary to the earlier face-offs with the police, which were unarmed and equipped only with riot gear.

The concern is high about any such possibility, as the senior leadership is aware of the consequences of a violent confrontation between the Rangers, which fall under the military's chain of command, and the Labbaik crowd.

'When the military and a mob come face to face, it ruins everything,' the senior security official said, alluding to examples from several other countries where a collision between the state and violent mobs has resulted in devastating fallouts.

The senior official also expressed concern that, given the weak domestic security landscape, any other external player and hostile intelligence agencies could try to exploit the situation. 'Some hidden hands can try to convince a large segment of the Barelvis that they are made to fight with the army,' the official said.

Given the highly combustible situation, officials say the government is treading on eggshells and has not closed the doors of talks and negotiations.

'I have given them the last chance,' the senior official said, adding that demands that fall within the legal purview and constitution of the country are open to discussion.

'A crackdown would be the last resort,' the senior intelligence official said.

Chapter 43

Talking with the Taliban

There is a need for national consensus on talks with militants

October 2021

Prime Minister Khan made an important revelation in an interview with a Turkish television news network on Friday that the government is in talks with some factions of the Taliban. The talks are being carried out in Afghanistan, the prime minister said, adding that the militants can be forgiven if they lay down their arms. Prime Minister Khan said that he has always been against a military solution and has advocated for political settlement and talks, especially in neighbouring Afghanistan. The same approach is to be carried out with the banned Tehreek-e-Taliban Pakistan (TTP) and other terrorist groups.

A faction under the leadership of Hafiz Gul Bahadur has declared a twenty-day ceasefire in North Waziristan, which is the first indication that peace negotiations are still ongoing. Officials say other groups are expected to join in soon.

Official quarters say that the negotiations will be within the confines of Pakistan's laws and constitution. The military operations have been successful and have achieved the desired results, a senior security official said. 'It is time now for the next step to bring this conflict to an end through political means,' the official said.

The peace talks will be held from a position of strength, officials here assert.

The desire to maintain peace and do away with any possibility of bloodshed is, of course, noble and praiseworthy. But there is a need for caution and deliberation, as we have been down this road before.

The country has earned peace after a protracted battle with the militants. The Pakistani army fought the terrorists valiantly and managed to wrest a large swath of tribal regions from them. It lost its finest officers and soldiers in this battle. The Pakistani people also endured the most terror attacks and faced them defiantly when the militants tried to make them cower and subdue them.

The successful military operations in the former tribal regions were hailed as having broken the proverbial backs of the militants. We were told that the militants could not regain their footholds and that their lethality had been neutralized. The decrease in terror attacks over the past few years speaks to the gains made against militant groups. But they were obviously not totally eliminated, and with the takeover of the Afghan Taliban, the militants in the country have reemerged and feel emboldened. The recent spate of attacks in the country's northwest and southwest regions is a troubling development.

The experiences of talk and negotiations with the militants do not provide much hope or optimism. Almost all peace talks and agreements with the militants resulted in their being further strengthened.

Just last month, the TTP rebuffed the amnesty offers by President Arif Alvi and Foreign Minister Shah Mahmood

Qureshi. The TTP vowed to continue with its armed ways unless its demands were accepted, and their version of religion implemented in the country. The militants do not accept the Pakistani constitution or the democratic system. A middle ground between both sides is hard to reach, given the stark differences and disagreements over the fundamentals.

Talking about peace talks with the militants casually is akin to being almost indifferent and insensitive to the sacrifices and pain suffered by the people. It also rings a bit hollow when state officials keep hammering at the international stage that the country's sacrifices of thousands of lives in the war against terrorism are not acknowledged.

This is not to suggest that efforts towards peace through talks are not worth trying. But there needs to be a more calculated, cohesive, and all-inclusive effort at the national level. The news about ongoing talks with the Taliban factions should not have come through a news channel's scoop but through a national consensus, a debate in the parliament, and the acceptance and willingness of a large majority of the people.

Chapter 44

Status Quo or Change

Imran Khan faces an internal revolt and opposition pressure builds up | Government insiders insist status quo will continue

January 2022

Frenetic speculation is once more engulfing the capital. The new round of rumours was fuelled further by a statement from Prime Minister Imran Khan, who termed the next three months crucial. The premier's heads-up might just have been about the economy, as the government is trying to stabilise its financial condition through painful measures amid a loud public outcry over inflation. A new agreement with the International Monetary Fund is also expected to be announced within this period. However, sensationalism is an essential staple of the political life of any capital, and Islamabad is no exception.

The timeframe of the next few months was therefore taken as some kind of make-or-break period during which the fate of the current government would be decided and sealed.

Opposition political parties have intensified their activity, and there has been a flurry of meetings between various party heads. An array of options about how Prime Minister Khan can be removed from power is being discussed. The PPP and PML–N have been in talks with much more urgency. The politics of rallies and long marches towards the capital is also making a comeback.

Much of the uncertainty also owes itself to the recent turbulence between the government and the military over the appointment of director-general ISI, the intelligence chief. Many observers concluded that the disagreement between the two power centres would not settle easily and would lead to far more lethal consequences.

The new intelligence chief, Lt Gen. Nadeem Ahmed Anjum, has also conducted himself in stark contrast to his predecessor. The high visibility has been drastically reduced and much of the work is being done in the shadows, true to the actual spirit of a spy agency.

The impression that the Establishment has now distanced itself from the ruling party is also compounded by the relative ease with which critical voices and opposition figures are finding airtime and the mea culpas of prominent talk show hosts, who were earlier staunch supporters of the ruling party.

Several opposition politicians now take delight in the alleged neutrality of the Establishment. Finally, they feel the government's Achilles heel has been exposed. There are also hushed whispers that disagreements persist over the next important appointment in the power calculus and that this will cast a dark and fateful cloud over the relationships between the major stakeholders.

Two scenarios have found more currency among the speculations about the political future:

a. no-confidence motion by the opposition political parties.
b. A forward bloc springs up in the next few months, citing growing public dissatisfaction over the rising cost of living and the government's alleged mishandling of the economy, and will force a change at the top.

Some opposition members say that in the absence of support from powerful quarters, the government will find it exceedingly difficult to maintain its already thin majority in parliament. The calculation proved to be correct in the long run as Khan was ousted through a vote of no-confidence in early 2022.

Ruling party members and allied partners, however, insisted that scratching beneath the surface and beyond the fevered pitch of talk about change, the opposition's optimism is misplaced. The status quo will continue, and there will be no change, they predict.

Disagreements between the PPP and PML–N over the new setup continue to stymie the opposition's momentum. PPP is still saddled with the governance failures of its past tenure. The power tussle in the PML–N has had a debilitating effect on the party's ability to come up with an effective and consistent narrative.

There have been grumblings by allied parties to the government, but they have been placated after a brief interlude of complaints and grievances. The allied political parties have reaffirmed their commitment to work with the ruling party in recent meetings with the prime minister.

A constant refrain among the ruling party and its allied members is about the lack of an alternative. Even if the powers-that-be want a change, their ability to enforce it with the tools of the past is greatly diminished, ruling party members think.

But true to every government in the twilight of its tenure, the treasury benches seem to have fallen into a false sense of security. The popularity of the ruling party has taken a sharp hit in recent months. Denials about plummeting popularity are self-delusional.

The tragedy of the ruling party is that before 2018, the PTI seemed understanding and empathetic about the public's concerns and, most of all, capable of solving those problems. Now, it sounds disconnected, tone-deaf, bungling and full of hubris. The Murree episode, in which twenty-two people lost their lives, is an example of how far-removed and unprepared the government was, not only in averting a tragedy but also in dealing with its aftermath.

The stormy session of the parliamentary committee on Thursday is an indication of the tough times ahead. Prime Minister Khan will increasingly face a hostile, impatient public, and pressure from within will build up.

Section III
(2022–2024)

Imran Khan's Bitter Falling out with
Gen. Bajwa and the Military

Chapter 45

The Cipher Mystery

*No foreign country sent a written threat |
Internal Foreign Office official communication
misconstrued as a threat to Imran's government*

March 2022

On 27 March, in front of a charged crowd of thousands of his supporters at a public rally in Islamabad, Prime Minister Khan alleged that a foreign conspiracy is underway in the country. Carefully reading a note, which the prime minister said he had written himself, Khan said local actors, at the behest of foreign players, were trying to topple his government.

Khan then took out a letter from his pocket and waved it in the air. He said he can reveal the contents, which substantiate a foreign conspiracy, off the record if someone doubts its veracity.

The accusation was indeed serious. But it has also raised serious questions about why the government kept sitting on the information and did not share it in meetings of the National Security Committee or inside the parliament. Opposition leader Shehbaz Sharif has jumped into the fray and said his party would have stood by Khan if the letter was presented before the parliament and if the threats were found to be real.

The federal cabinet has not spoken with a single voice on the issue.

Shah Mehmood Qureshi, the foreign minister, has said that the letter's contents were shared with the security establishment. However, Qureshi told the local news media that the contents could not be shared with journalists off the record. Sheikh Rashid Ahmed, the interior minister, totally distanced himself from the letter, claiming that he is unaware of its existence.

Federal ministers Asad Umar and Fawad Chaudhry stressed that a letter containing threats to the PTI government does exist. They claimed that the letter mentioned the no-confidence motion against Prime Minister Khan and warned of grave consequences. Umar declined to reveal the source of the letter but added that the government could show the contents of the letter to the country's chief justice.

Background discussions with official and diplomatic sources have revealed that no foreign country has given any written threat to the Pakistani government. But Pakistan's former ambassador to the US, Asad M. Khan, had communicated to Islamabad the unease of American officials about the troubled bilateral relations.

Senior officials, however, deny that any written threat was received, and that the communication was 'something trivial' and a 'case of misconstruing a conversation'.

Prime Minister Khan has been railing against the United States in recent rallies, accusing his political opponents of being 'slaves of America'. Anti-American sentiment has long been a staple of Khan's politics, and he criticized the decision of former president Pervez Musharraf to side with the US in the campaign against terrorism.

Khan had also been a vociferous critic of the US policy of using drones to target militants in the country's northwestern tribal regions. He led several protest rallies against the use of drones, which often resulted in collateral damage.

Historically, Pakistan and the US have had a relationship that fluctuated between close cooperation and latent hostility. The defence sides of both countries have enjoyed close cooperation and remain strong. Pakistan was once considered an important non-NATO ally of the United States. As far back as the 1950s, Pakistan enjoyed close cooperation with the West in the Southeast Asia Treaty Organization (SEATO) and Central Treaty Organization (CENTO) accords.

Pakistan has a vast and thriving diaspora in the US and several European countries. Russia and China are culturally more alien to Pakistanis than the West.

Prime Minister Khan says he wants to pursue an independent foreign policy. He has also stressed that he cannot partner with any country in any act of war.

Supporters of Khan's point of view say the country has been treated unfairly by the United States. The feeling is, in fact, prevalent across a vast swath of the country.

Khan's recent visit to Moscow just as the Russian troops were invading Ukraine has raised serious concerns in Washington, D.C., and European capitals.

Official sources confirm that Khan declined advice from Jake Sullivan, President Biden's national security adviser, not to visit Moscow at a time when diplomatic tensions between Moscow and Western countries were peaking.

Under Khan's government, relations with the United States have reached a nadir. This is despite the fact that Khan had a good relationship with former US President Donald Trump. But with the Biden administration, relations have witnessed a chill.

The fact that Biden has not made a telephone call to Khan has caused a lot of unease in Islamabad.

The Pakistan–US relationship is so troubled and damaged right now that US officials feel it cannot be repaired under the Khan government.

Analysts say the damage to the bilateral relationship can be mitigated.

'The US continues to see the Pakistani military as such a key interlocutor. So, relations with the civilian leadership may get strained by Khan's anti-West and conspiratorial rhetoric. But mil-to-military ties are not necessarily impacted,' said Michael Kugelman, a South Asia expert and deputy director of the Asia Programme.

Given the risk to relations, Kugelman stated, 'I wouldn't be surprised if Khan's rhetoric turns the army off.'

'The army seems more receptive to continued partnership with the US than does the civilian leadership,' he said.

In August 2023, Pakistani authorities opened a criminal investigation against Khan over charges of leaking the classified diplomatic cable. The investigation was widely known as 'the Cipher case'.

In late October 2023, Asad Majeed, the former Pakistani ambassador to Washington, submitted a damning statement before the country's Federal Investigation Agency, stating that his cable did not contain any reference to a 'threat' or 'conspiracy.' Any mention of these terms was a 'political conclusion' drawn by the Khan government, the former diplomat said. He also stressed that the Cipher episode cast doubts on the integrity of Pakistan's communication system, the credibility of its diplomats and the future of diplomatic reporting culture.

State   Vs   Imran Khan Niazi and others
Case FIR No. 06/2023 dated 15/08/2023, u/s 5, 9 of Official Secrets Act 1923 r/w section 34 PPC

STATEMENT OF DR. ASAD MAJEED KHAN, FORMER AMBASSADOR OF PAKISTAN TO THE UNITED STATES U/S 161 CR.P.C

I was an officer in BS-22 from Foreign Service of Pakistan and I served as Foreign Secretary in Ministry of Foreign Affairs of Pakistan, Islamabad from December 2022 till my retirement. Prior to this posting, I was Ambassador of Pakistan in USA from January 2019 to March 2022. I had invited the Assistant Secretary for South & Central Asian Affairs under US States Department Mr. Donald Lu on 07.03.2022. It was a preplanned lunch hosted by me in the Pakistan House in Washington for the U.S. team dealing with Pakistan, which was scheduled, at about 1230 Hrs. It lasted for one and a half hour.

The invitees / participants of this lunch were Assistant Secretary of State Mr. Donald Lu accompanied / assisted by Deputy Assistant Secretary of State Lesslie Viguerie. From our side, it was myself, Defence Attache Brig. Nauman Awan, Deputy Chief of Mission Naveed Bokhari and Counsellor Political Qasim Mohiuddin. Both sides were aware that the conversation was being minuted, as is the standard practice on such occasions. There was no special occasion. It was part of the regular consultations held with U.S. interlocutors, including the White House, Department of Defence, USTR in addition to the State Department. This was a practice adopted during Covid because of the U.S. side's inability to host meetings at their premises. The conversation covered the whole range of issues in our bilateral relations.

Consequently, communication was sent to Islamabad covering lunch. The subject communication was a Cypher Telegram addressed to the Foreign Secretary, who then shared its copies with others in line with his competence. It was sent through our secret coded communication system, used for correspondence between Foreign Missions of Pakistan and the Ministry of Foreign Affairs in Islamabad, in compliance to the documented instructions of the Cabinet Division.

Chapter 46

DG ISI, the Intelligence Chief, Steps into the Picture

October 2022

In an unexpected turn of events, the country's intelligence chief and the military spokesperson assumed the centre stage of a live press briefing this month. This marked an unmistakable pivot in the armed forces' approach to the political quagmire that had been simmering since the unceremonious exit of ex-prime minister, Khan, in April. It was an unprecedented sight: the director-general ISI, the intelligence chief, presenting himself to the probing glances and pointed questions of live television reporters. It had never happened earlier in the country's history.

Imran Khan, the ousted prime minister, had for months been on a relentless political campaign, his influence cascading across a wide stratum of voters. Yet, the previous ruling party had also let loose a veritable flood of derision and scorn against the military top rungs. High-ranking intelligence officers were disrespected, referred to as Mr X, Mr Y and Dirty Harry, as Khan, irate about losing political backing, attempted to influence the security apparatus. His once allies and supporters were now branded as betrayers, accused of enabling a 'regime change'.

Such a barrage of accusations was starting to erode the mystique and enigma that contributed to the institution's pride and honour. The director general of the ISI, Lt Gen. Nadeem Ahmed Anjum, took it upon himself to step forward and address the matter.

When the head of intelligence breaks cover, it not only signifies the military's sense of pressure but also signals a possible shift in policy. This press briefing wasn't about placating the PTI. That was no longer possible. It was intended to deliver a wider political message to the masses. The director-general of ISI unveiled Khan's hypocritical dealings, disclosing his covert late-night meetings with loyal followers and intelligence and security officers, in an attempt to regain the favour of Army Chief Gen. Qamar Javed Bajwa by extending his tenure indefinitely.

Lt Gen. Anjum emphasized his commitment to accountability, clarifying that its scale should not be determined by the extent of his, and his organization's, support for a political faction. Lt Gen. Anjum and Lt Gen. Babar Iftikhar, the military spokesperson, reiterated the institution's decision to remain 'apolitical', a resolution reached in the wake of the Senate elections the previous year.

The briefing held a dual message at its core. The PTI was informed that peaceful political activities were not an issue. However, attempts to incite anarchy and civil discord would not be tolerated; only demands within the constitutional framework were acceptable. This announcement essentially squashed the potential of the Long March, Imran Khan's proposed protest rally, to effect a change in the civil government via the threat of violent protest.

Moreover, the briefing highlighted that the outlined policy would be adhered to by the incoming army chief. The public appearances of the two commanders suggested that the military had grown weary of exercising restraint, which was being misinterpreted as internal division or frailty. That misapprehension was dispelled; now was the time for candid dialogue, to be followed by firm action.

Imran Khan responded to this extraordinary press briefing with his own brand of defiance and retaliation. Initiating the protest movement on Friday, 28 October, he adopted a menacing tone towards the ISI chief, and for the first time named other senior ISI officials in public, accusing them of torturing PTI leaders, veering from his previous indirect insinuations.

The real implications of the press briefing and the standoff between Khan and the military will become evident in the forthcoming weeks.

While some observers critiqued the decision to shed the cloak of secrecy and step into the spotlight, others, including security officials, deemed it a necessary step to 'inject reality into a post-truth era'.

One certainty remains: the political face-off that has held the country in its grasp for months is inching dangerously close to the point of head-on collision.

Chapter 47

Imran and the Military

A confrontation with dangerous consequences

November 2022

One afternoon in May 2018, I stepped into Aleem Khan's office in Gulberg, Lahore. I had to interview Imran Khan, and Aleem's plush and tastefully decorated office was the venue. The General Election was just around the corner. There was an air of excitement and anticipation in the air. 'Nicely done!' I complimented Aleem on the decor as we waited and made small talk in one of the seating areas. Aleem smiled and said he brought most of the furniture from Dubai. At that time, Aleem was considered close to Imran, along with Jahangir Khan Tareen, and their financial support was vital for the political party. After a short wait, Khan arrived, dressed in his signature crisp white shalwar qameez. 'Get me a coffee,' Khan told someone in the bevy of people following him. A takeaway coffee was quickly brought in from a nearby Dunkin' Donuts. Imran took a sip as we sat down in Aleem's upstairs office.

I noticed a certain buoyancy in Khan that day, quite different from my past interactions with him. It was as if he was assured of winning the upcoming election. The primary reason was that the powerful military establishment had thrown its weight behind Khan. I prodded him about this support in the interview and detailed it in the article I wrote for the *New York Times* titled 'Imran Khan warms to Pakistan's military. His political fortune rose.'

Khan subsequently won the August 2018 elections, and for the most part of his three-and-a-half-year rule, he enjoyed a close, almost unprecedented, working relationship with the military.

But today, Imran and the military find themselves on different sides. The public fallout after Imran was ousted from power earlier in 2022 has been bitter, loud, and messy. In recent interviews, Imran Khan has said that Aleem Khan, the ally-turned-foe, is one of the two main reasons he had disagreements with the army chief, Gen. Bajwa. This is only partially true, and the disagreements ran far deeper.

Khan's challenge to his powerful benefactors has set the stage for a confrontation like never before. Imran feels unstoppable because of the unwavering public support, and he has increased the stakes every time the military has tried to subdue him. He has accused a senior intelligence general, apart from his main political rivals, of being behind the gun attack on his life last month. In a letter to President Alvi, Khan declared an open season on the country's intelligence chief and the chief spokesperson of the army, seeking action against both generals for a public press conference against him. While Khan has taken aim at these officers, it is obvious that his real target is elsewhere.

In public appearances, Khan has launched powerful tirades against the role of the security establishment in the country's politics. He has questioned the overgrown influence and the overarching role. But many are left confused about the real motive. Has Imran become the torchbearer of civilian supremacy, or is he just blackmailing the military into submission by raising the constant spectre of violence and mass protests? Even Khan is hard-pressed to clearly answer this question, as was evident by his recent interview with TRT TV.

The press conference by the director-general of ISI and the director-general of ISPR revealed that while Khan had a menacingly confrontational public posture, he was simultaneously trying to mend fences backstage.

Some can see Khan's strategy as effective realpolitik. But Khan's brinkmanship has also pushed things over the edge and can be seen as an escalation that risks dangerous consequences. His unrelenting protest campaign that questions the neutrality of the military has set off a wave of public discontent and widened the fissures that already exist in the country's polity. It is a genie that even Imran cannot put back in the bottle.

The new chief will be faced with an immediate set of challenges, with hardly any time to settle down. The bitter political residue of the past few months will weigh heavily, and Imran's politics can exert pressure on the apolitical vows of the top brass. Even if the new chief decides to placate Khan in some way, history tells us that he will find it impossible to cede the proverbial power to a civilian challenger.

Chapter 48

General Bajwa: From Benefactor to Pariah

November 2022

Shortly before his retirement, Gen. Bajwa asked his colleagues why the public was not fully supporting him. There had been an unprecedented barrage of vitriol and criticism heaped on Gen. Bajwa, spearheaded by supporters of the PTI, upset at losing their government earlier this year. The profane language used by the public on social media and retired army officials in WhatsApp groups was once unimaginable.

Discussing the possible reasons for this, a senior official compared the situation to a fast-moving truck where the prime mover changes the direction abruptly, but the loaded container moves on due to inertia, suggesting that Gen. Bajwa and others never shared with the public, especially the serving and retired officers, how badly their project was failing. And due to utmost frustration, when the military leadership decided not to render further ('unconstitutional') support to PTI's non-performing regime, the wider audience was not on board. Imran readily crafted a popular, sellable narrative, which was lapped up by the public, unaware of the background.

The exchange illustrated the dilemma and the downturn Gen. Bajwa faced in the twilight of his career as the army chief. For years, since becoming the army chief in 2016, he enjoyed unbridled power and greatly influenced the country's domestic and foreign policies. Khan, the former prime minister, showered lavish praise on Gen. Bajwa, complimenting him for the support lent to his government since the 2018 elections. But once out of power, Imran and his supporters tried to portray Gen. Bajwa as a pariah. The PML–N saw Gen. Bajwa in the same light but watered down its criticism only after the current coalition government was eased into power.

Gen. Bajwa's tenure as chief started on an optimistic and ambitious note. The then prime minister, Nawaz Sharif, was hopeful that the general's support for the civilian government during the 2014 protests by PTI and his vows for harmonious civil–military relations meant well for the future. But the *Dawn Leaks'* fallout and Panama Leaks investigations were used to browbeat PML–N and dent the relationship to such an extent that by the end of 2017, Nawaz Sharif was not only out of power but subsequently jailed and battling for political survival. Those were heady days for Gen. Bajwa and his core team. They tried to rearrange the political drawing board, winnow the electoral field in favour of Khan's party, and chart a new political landscape for the country.

Much of it was well-intentioned, they stressed. Years of political and economic instability and the hold of dynastic politicians on power saw little progress for the country. Khan was given a rare welcome at the GHQ in 2018, and the new government tried to make a grand new beginning under the supervision of Gen. Bajwa and through handling by the former intelligence chief, Lt Gen. Faiz Hamid.

I remember how in 2019 a former senator used to breathlessly tell me about the future in which Khan's rivals had no space anymore, the 'looted wealth kept offshore' was to be brought back to give the economy a jump-start, and how a presidential system was on the horizon.

In 2018, the army chief's domestic and foreign policy agenda was made public as the ambitious 'Bajwa Doctrine'. But such a policy shift needed the sustained support of the civilian government and much to the dismay of Gen. Bajwa and his team, 'Project Imran' failed spectacularly.

The Khan government differed from Gen. Bajwa on many counts, especially over governance, failed to revive the economy, and handled foreign policy in an amateur manner. The singular focus on targeting and jailing the political opposition while ignoring the economy and governance polarised the country like never before and deepened the differences between Imran and the army chief.

Gen. Bajwa's decision to seek an extension of his term in 2019 made matters worse. It bred resentment among the top brass. The flamboyance and discernible public ambitions of Lt Gen. Faiz to become the next army chief and Khan's vows to help achieve these ambitions further emboldened the rivals, both political and in the security establishment.

Gen. Bajwa was also confronted with the accruing residue of his long time in office. His plans to hand over military-run commercial enterprises, which were gradually running into losses, to civilians were met with disgruntlement and opposition by retired generals, who saw these posts as their post-retirement right and tried to cling on. Gen. Bajwa oversaw several selection boards for the senior officers, and those left out of promotions started to grumble.

Several retired generals, who were passed over to be the chief in 2016 or other coveted positions in recent years and had political ambitions or saw Gen. Bajwa's ascension due to factors other than merit, coalesced around Imran, and the former spy chief's network within the system also created a parallel competing structure. The lack or absence of any action against the former spy chief, who allegedly provided an 'insider's view about the establishment's behaviour dynamics' to Khan, baffled many. Some felt that Gen. Bajwa was compelled by certain considerations or even tacitly supported his protege. Others felt it was a sign of his weakened hold on power.

As Gen. Bajwa confronted these internal challenges, he decided to withdraw support for Khan's government by February 2021. Khan's attempt to assert himself, without realizing that he had little control over the actual levers of power, saw the relationship between him and Gen. Bajwa fracture beyond repair in October 2021, especially over Lt Gen. Faiz's future. Khan's government unravelled quickly, with the lack of support from the Deep State becoming its Achilles heel, which culminated in the success of the no-confidence vote in April this year.

Now, Gen. Bajwa was no longer the benefactor but a villain in the eyes of Khan and his supporters. Never has an army chief been bashed so openly and so insolently. Gen. Bajwa exhibited restraint for several months, partly due to the changing environment in the country and partly because of his temperament. He has an immense tolerance threshold. The general also has a habit of talking up a storm in private meetings and often expresses his views and opinions in a very frank, uninhibited manner.

While Gen. Bajwa's domestic ambitions in politics were dashed to the ground, his record on the military and foreign policy fronts proved to be relatively better. He managed to continue the successes of his predecessors against militancy, and terrorism was significantly reduced under his watch. He also managed to throw a ring around radical and militant groups and oversaw the successful delisting of Pakistan from the Financial Action Task Force grey list. Furthermore, he also oversaw much of the completion of the fencing of the Afghan and Iranian borders.

The military under Gen. Bajwa saw some success against India in the wake of the 2019 Pulwama crisis when both countries to the brink of a full-scale war. The capture of an Indian air force pilot tilted the balance in Pakistan's favour, and his subsequent release was seen as a noble gesture for peace by Pakistan. However many people felt that the real credit went to the Pakistan Air Force (PAF) and its operational prowess. After the Balakot air force showdown, PAF felt shortchanged and subsequently expanded its own media directorate to showcase its accomplishments.

Gen. Bajwa also personally oversaw the opening of the Kartarpur Corridor, which provides Sikh pilgrims easy access to Pakistan to visit their holy places. He also managed the successful implementation of a ceasefire on the Line of Control, much to the relief of the Kashmiri population. Many in the country, however, felt that Pakistan's response to India's annexation of Kashmir in 2019 was lacking.

His plans for normalization of ties with India and the gradual opening of trade were scuttled by Khan's cabinet, wary of domestic political compulsions. Moeed Yusuf, the former national security advisor, made a bumbling response about Khan's decision to first support and then withdraw plans for limited trade with India. It was because Khan made the decision to support as the commerce minister and backed off as the prime minister, Yusuf said. Such a decision-making process would bamboozle anyone.

Gen. Bajwa tried to avoid a total breakdown of the country's relationship with the United States but was undone by the Taliban takeover of Kabul. He also signalled his willingness to ally with the US and Europe over Russia's invasion of Ukraine, a sign that the Pakistani security establishment did not want to cut its traditional alliance with the Americans.

But like several army chiefs in the past, Gen. Bajwa also discovered the limits of power and the extent to which he could wield it. His bitter and public fallout with Khan is an instructive lesson. The 'hybrid experiment' could not deliver, and its collapse has cast a shadow over Gen. Bajwa's legacy. The questions about the burgeoning finances of his family have also raised eyebrows, though Gen. Bajwa and his family deny any wrongdoing.

As Gen. Bajwa doffed his uniform on 29 November 2022, some senior PTI politicians, who used to brown-nose and ingratiate themselves in their meetings when Gen. Bajwa was the chief, quickly took to Twitter to denounce him. It was quite hypocritical but also indicative of the viciousness of politics. Gen. Bajwa must have felt bitter and let down his proteges, both civil and non-civilian, and turned on him.

Gen. Bajwa's body language during the change of command ceremony in Rawalpindi bore testimony to what was echoing inside his heart and mind. Soldiers aspire for and cherish their image zealously, but Gen. Bajwa's public image was destroyed by the very people to whom he provided immense benefits.

It is a fate that he now must contend with. Power, especially the one enjoyed by army chiefs in Pakistan, is intoxicating and can be equally crushing when it slips away.

Chapter 49

Double Game

Gen. Bajwa accused of playing all sides

December 2022

Suddenly, there is a deluge of news about former army chief Gen. Bajwa's 'double game'. Several analysts claim that Gen. Bajwa played all sides before his retirement and tried to get another extension. By varying accounts, it is now being claimed that Gen. Bajwa tried to get a six-month extension so he could salvage his battered public image by overseeing another election, a key demand of the PTI after his removal from office and repair the broken ties with Khan.

It is not the first time that Pakistani generals have been accused of playing a double game. The playbook of the double game involves squaring off all sides against one another while maintaining leverage to extract maximum benefit. It is the classic divide-and-rule strategy. The term was popularized by the Americans, especially after 2006, when the Taliban insurgency inside Afghanistan suddenly gained strength and the Pakistani military was accused of supporting both the coalition forces and the Taliban, a charge denied by Pakistani officials.

The speculation about Bajwa's double game grew stronger after Chaudhry Moonis Elahi, the son of the Punjab chief minister, made a disclosure last week that the decision to join Khan was based on a nudge by the former army chief.

Gen. Bajwa is also accused of restraining the coalition government from arresting Khan after the April vote of no-confidence. This allowed Khan the space to extend his protest campaign, hog TV and mobile screens, and build on his narrative of being a victim of a grand conspiracy. The freedom to act culminated in his electoral wins in several by-elections and dented the ruling coalition's mandate to govern. It is true that soon after taking over the government in early 2022, several PML–N leaders, notably Javed Latif, publicly expressed frustration with the way their hands were tied in dealing with the PTI.

The public defence of Gen. Bajwa by the Chaudhrys, an influential political family from Punjab, seems to be an attempt at damage control. It punctures the narrative of PTI about Gen. Bajwa being the sole villain, but paradoxically, it still paints the former chief in a questionable manner. Was he merely advising the Chaudhrys in a frank, selfless manner or was he playing all sides to his advantage?

The double-game interpretation provides a simplified version of the events that took place in the last couple of months. The reality can be complex, even contradictory. All sides indulge in skullduggery and subterfuge, as happens in power politics and competing forces do not necessarily overlap all the time.

Punjab fell into the lap of the PTI in July after the Supreme Court's decision on the vote count. And there was a lot of unease both in Rawalpindi and Aabpara about the court's verdict, which was deemed contradictory and an overreach by the justices.

Gen. Bajwa, in the last leg of his long six-year tenure, was substantially weakened and faced growing pressure, criticism and opposition from the top brass.

There were few takers for yet another extension. The idea was essentially floated as a last-ditch ploy by Lt Gen. Faiz Hamid, discernibly the most ambitious aspirant to the army chief's position. But the real aim was to ensure that Gen. Faiz himself stayed in the running for chief until April 2023.

Gen. Faiz was unlike his predecessors and, comparatively speaking, proved to be a more resilient and deft intel operator. For example, Lt Gen. Rizwan Akhtar, one of Faiz's predecessors, failed to get an extension for his boss. Faiz managed to get one extension for his boss, Gen. Bajwa, in 2019 (and the pressure and stress were so great that it affected his health; one evening he collapsed on the tennis court, according to his colleagues).

Much of Faiz's mystique and reputation are owed to his long stint at the ISI and his way of dealing. Sharp and incisive, he was not shy of coming to the forefront and taking matters into his own hands. His dealmaking, though, was questioned by his critics, who accused him of reneging on agreements without batting an eyelid. Gen. Faiz had a peculiar way of dealing with his opponents: he would almost crush them and then cut a deal.

And yet, despite his reputation as a go-getter and a master strategist, Gen. Faiz remained unable to turn his ambition to be the chief into a reality. He did shake up politics like never before.

The relationship between Gen. Faiz and Gen. Bajwa was most curious. Faiz continued to serve the prime minister's interests until October 2021, despite the apparent orders of his boss. Faiz dabbled in politics even after the top brass vowed to remain apolitical. Still, Gen. Bajwa remained unwilling or unable to keep him in check. Some described the inaction as the result of both being partners in the original sin. Some people have even speculated that both, in fact, played a masterful double game. They cultivated an image of differences in public, but in private they continued to shield and protect one another's interests.

Gen. Bajwa, however, did not really have the wherewithal to force another extension. His best bet was to have a chief of his own choice. But this attempt failed to see the light of day, as both the Sharifs and Asif Ali Zardari were wary of the continuity of the 'Bajwa Doctrine' and resisted all attempts. A strong group within the Establishment had also had enough with the way the army, under Bajwa and Faiz, had been dragged into muddy politics and wanted a clean break.

The run-up to 29 November, the day Gen. Bajwa doffed his uniform, was a game of nerves, and Prime Minister Shehbaz Sharif, holding the authority to appoint the new chief, was really the ace in the pack.

Chapter 50

General Musharraf: A Deep but Controversial Imprint

The former military ruler dies at seventy-nine

February 2023

Former military ruler Gen. Musharraf has left an undeniably deep but controversial imprint on the country's politics. His era was eventful, with far-reaching consequences. The controversies of Gen. Musharraf's rule will overshadow and define his legacy. Political unrest and the militant backlash spawned by his policies are still present in the country.

Gen. Musharraf had a forceful presence on the global stage and led the country through a turbulent time after the 11 September 2001, terror attacks in New York. The critics, who accuse him of caving to the US pressure at that time, are unaware of the gravity of the post-9/11 situation. The US initially hailed him as an indispensable ally in the war against terrorism.

Liberal policies and the opening of the economy by Gen. Musharraf paved the way for a new consumer class. Much of the good of his initial years in power was, however, undone by the 2007 political and security turmoil. This led to his ignominious fall from power in 2008. In the twilight years of his rule, Gen.

Musharraf had become such a global and domestic liability that the 'deep state', led by Gen. Kayani, removed him from power, using the façade of a political movement.

Gen. Musharraf made a failed attempt at carving out a comeback. But his homecoming in 2013 was unremarkable; he ended up being hauled before the courts, faced a plethora of legal cases, and had to return to a life of exile in Dubai. His political foes managed to make a return to power, while Musharraf, devoid of his military fatigues, was pushed to the sidelines.

Gen. Musharraf was a reluctant coup leader. The 1999 military takeover was an institutional response. It was triggered by brewing resentment within the top brass over the treatment of army chiefs by former prime minister Nawaz Sharif prior to Gen. Musharraf. But once Gen. Musharraf took over, he found it difficult to let go of power.

Personally he was charming, with a pleasant disposition. His candour was often persuasive and even delightful. He liked attractive, social company and knew how to enjoy life. Some people look back on his initial years in office with a certain nostalgia. Senior army officers and civilian officials who worked with him talk fondly about his leadership style. Gen. Musharraf made bold decisions. Some turned out well; others went awry. 'Decisiveness' in his personality was a defining trait and a big part of his legacy.

But the Kargil debacle of 1999, the increasing Taliban militancy in the country, the assassinations of Benazir Bhutto and Nawab Akbar Bugti under his watch, the assault on the constitution, and the civil–military imbalance that has only been exacerbated since his rule cast a dark cloud on the public's memory. Though he wanted to be remembered as a benevolent military ruler, the sharp changes in Pakistani society over the past few years will deny him that place.

The news of Gen. Musharraf's death comes at a time of heightened political unrest and societal fissures. The military's popularity has dipped since the last army chief, Gen. Bajwa's controversial political role and standoff with Khan's party raised questions about the military's role in politics, even among those who used to support it ardently.

Chapter 51

From Praise to Blame

Gen. Bajwa's standing shifts dramatically in Imran Khan's world

February 2023

Khan's politics has become a game of whack-a-mole: every time you think you have a handle on what he stands for, he pops up with a completely different position. Backtracking has become a defining feature of his leadership style, and it seems that with each passing day, he manages to outdo himself in terms of inconsistencies and U-turns. At this point, it is nearly impossible to keep track of all the positions Khan has taken.

Khan has now shifted the blame for his ouster from the US to Gen. Qamar Javed Bajwa, the former army chief. The irony of Khan's shift in blame is not lost on anyone. For years, and not long before his ouster in April last year, Imran kept praising Gen. Bajwa. But now, the former army chief is the focus of Imran's bitter tirades.

It cannot be denied that Gen. Bajwa has had a controversial role in Pakistan's political and military landscape. And, with each passing day, a new controversy seems to emanate from this convoluted situation. The latest episode is the alleged phone call between the former army chief and a talk-show host. Gen. Bajwa allegedly confessed to taping his meetings with Imran Khan, who is now demanding that President Arif Alvi initiate an inquiry against his former benefactor.

The ugly fallout between Gen. Bajwa and Imran Khan is taking on the dimensions of a soap opera. Khan used to openly gush about Gen. Bajwa and describe the general as a staunch believer in democracy and a supporter of his government. But since last April,

Gen. Bajwa's standing has shifted dramatically in Imran Khan's world: from the finest pro-democracy army chief to evil incarnate.

Imran Khan is also finding it hard to come to terms with his public image as an anti-American politician. Khan has been known for his anti-American sentiments and his outspoken criticism of US foreign policy. He blamed the US for many of the ills plaguing the country, including support for military rulers, the use of drones in the tribal regions, and militancy inside Pakistan and neighbouring Afghanistan. Imran Khan's latest assertion that Gen. Bajwa 'somehow convinced the Americans that he is anti-American' is amusing to say the least.

The Khan–Bajwa acrimony illustrates the complex relationship between the military and politics in Pakistan. However, what is most striking about Khan's approach is the lack of guilt or remorse that he shows when he changes his position. The way he does so seems effortless and without any regard for the consequences or impact on his credibility.

The constant flip-flops of Imran Khan are now seen as a sign of a lack of commitment to his own beliefs. The constant stream of U-turns has had a detrimental effect on the country's political fibre, which is already fragile and prone to instability. Increasingly, people are cynical about politics. Many of those who thought Imran was different from traditional politicians are now forced to reconsider their belief in him.

Despite all this, it is no surprise that Khan's base continues to lap up whatever he says, even if it is hugely contradictory. Due to his charisma and passion for what he does, his supporters are willing to overlook his inconsistencies because they continue to believe that he has their best interests at heart.

However, this kind of blind loyalty can be dangerous. It reinforces a culture of misinformation and undermines the democratic process.

On the other end of the political spectrum, when Shehbaz Sharif became the prime minister after the no-confidence vote in parliament last April, there were lofty expectations of him. His record of accomplishment in Punjab as a development-oriented, super-efficient administrator had earned him a reputation as a leader who could deliver results.

But Prime Minister Shehbaz Sharif has lagged in providing the kind of inspiring leadership that was expected of him in these tumultuous times. It is evident that the challenges of a coalition government have weighed heavily on the prime minister. Prime Minister Shehbaz Sharif has been on the move, but meaningful progress has been missing.

Meanwhile, rifts within the PML–N are being exacerbated. Miftah Ismail, the former finance minister, has been trying to reimagine the world of Pakistani politics. His reaction to his unceremonious ouster as finance minister has been gradual and has gained steam and pungency in recent weeks. Many, though, are left wondering if his foray into the world of re-imagination of country's politics is a personal effort or resulted from a nudge from powerful quarters—as a testing of the waters exercises for a future national or technocratic setup.

Shahid Khaqan Abbasi is also on a different tangent from his political party and is one of the biggest advocates for a national unity government. He acts as prime minister, but the Sharifs did not go through the troubles of the Bajwa–Faiz–Khan years to simply hand it over to Abbasi.

In all this mix, there has been a steady stream of appointments of special advisors to the prime minister. These appointments reek of a certain tone-deafness characteristic of PML–N and a disconnect from the street. The frequent foreign trips of the Prime Minister have also been criticized by his opponents.

Prime Minister Shehbaz Sharif has been most troubled by the impression that his leadership style lacks decisiveness. There has been a widespread feeling that he has dithered in taking tough decisions, and, therefore, the government has been unable to move forward with a clear direction even though the agenda has been obvious right from the start.

This lack of meaningful action has caused frustration among the party base and eroded the trust and credibility of the government. Prime Minister Shehbaz Sharif's major challenge is to steer the country to the next elections, whenever the coalition leadership finally decides to hold them. In the run-up to the elections, Prime Minister Shehbaz Sharif also needs to provide a cushion for his own party from the grinding inflation that is going to hit the electorate in the coming weeks and months. A government cannot accomplish this daunting task without clear thinking and a firm hand.

Despite all the shortcomings that have defined Khan's agitational politics, he remains a potent threat to the ruling alliance. Attempts to have Khan disqualified or thrown in jail will only add to his popularity and provide further fuel to his narrative of being a victim and outsider to the traditional political realm.

The challenges for Prime Minister Shehbaz Sharif are mounting, and the coming few weeks will be critical for the government. They will determine the course of the future, not only for Shehbaz Sharif as prime minister but for the political survival of Khan as well.

Chapter 52

Mystery about Jinnah House Attack

A Mob Set Fire to the Lahore Corps Commander House on 9 May

May 2023

The Jinnah House, or the Lahore Corps Commander's House, bore the mark of Pakistan's our national heritage. It was once the abode of the founding father, Quaid-e-Azam, before the 1947 partition.

Contents of two viral WhatsApp voice notes, allegedly propagated by family acquaintances of the former Lahore Corps Commander, present a perplexing account of events on May 9, when protesters belonging to Khan's political party entered the ordinarily highly secure military cantonment neighbourhood of Lahore and many other military installations across the country. Once inside the Lahore cantonment, the protesters forced entry into the top military commander's official residence. They ransacked it and set it on fire.

Lt Gen. Salman Fayaz Ghani allegedly ordered his troops to allow the PTI mob free rein within the cantonment, inclusive of his official residence and brigade headquarters. This enabled the mob to indulge in looting, vandalism and arson.

It was reported that he assisted his family in seeking refuge in a neighbouring residence owned by a relative of Chief Justice Umer Atta Bandial, escaping via ladder, while he made a beeline through the main entrance.

In this web of allegations, a disconcerting question emerges: if the corps commander indeed had sympathies with the PTI mob, why did they publicly ridicule him after ravaging his residence? In a widely circulated video, Imran Khan's nephew, Hassan Niazi, is seen parading a pair of khaki trousers, claiming they belonged to the fleeing Lt Gen. Ghani. Laughter erupts as Hassan discloses the corps commander's waist measurement of fifty.

The narrative from a viral female WhatsApp voice note suggests an ill-prepared Lahore Corps Commander. A video revealing the general in sweatpants, sporting a panicked countenance while addressing the mob, corroborates this narrative. The anonymous female alleged that the general found himself entrapped, his calls for assistance to senior officials ignored. Rumours circulated those key personnel ranging from the Chief of Staff to the Quick Response Force, junior officers, police, and field intelligence unit had all mysteriously absented themselves under some sinister design. This claim further taints the image of the commander, questioning his operational command over his forces.

The female voice note portrays Lt Gen. Ghani not as a corps commander, one of the country's most potent military positions, but as a gentle, naive husband and father, caught unawares amidst familial tranquillity by a sudden assault from the mob.

A crucial question arises as to why he failed to foresee, pre-empt, and safeguard vital state institutions. The query here is not whether he should have employed force, firing upon protestors, but rather why he fell short in his duty to secure military installations, an obligation for which he had been trained, remunerated, and accorded privileges by the state for over thirty years. Speculations abound, suggesting that his actions were influenced by certain familial ties.

Irrespective of how one dissects the incident, Lt Gen. Ghani's actions do not cast a favourable light on him.

Lt Gen. Ghani was subsequently court-martialled and dismissed from service. (More details in 'Major Shake-Up in Military' chapter.)

Chapter 53

Political Turmoil Reaches a Crescendo

11 May 2023

The Corps Commander's House in Lahore has long been an inaccessible and highly coveted place for many locals. To a passerby, it inspired both awe and fear. However, on Tuesday 9 May, thousands of Khan supporters breached the security barriers and entered the cantonment, converging on the house. They proceeded to smash windows, and as security officials retreated, the protesters ransacked the premises as if it were enemy territory.

The destruction was not limited to furniture, doors, and windows; many of the protesters seized items for themselves, such as decorative pieces, an expensive golf set, and even cold strawberries from the kitchen. One man took a peacock, while another absconded with a plate of 'qorma'.

The protesters, who were furious over the arrest of their leader, Khan, believed that their act of ransacking was justified. According to one female protester, everything on the property was purchased with public money, while the peacock enthusiast claimed that the luxurious residence was only possible because of the people's taxes. These were truly unprecedented scenes, with the protesters setting the property ablaze as the evening shadows lengthened.

Earlier in the day, hundreds of protesters attempted to breach the gates of the army's GHQ in Rawalpindi, an act that had only been carried out once before by Taliban militants in 2009. However, Imran Khan's arrest has provoked such fury and outrage across the country that military installations, government offices, and other public property have become targets of mob violence.

It should not come as a surprise, really. Khan had himself warned of such dire consequences.

The military has released its initial response to the current disorder and violence across the country. It cautioned that any further attacks on military installations would result in tough action and highlighted that the troops' self-control the previous day was deliberate to prevent any attempts to instigate a civil war. The military condemned elements within Khan's party who mask their hunger for power as a democratic struggle and reiterated that legal measures would be taken against arsonists and rioters.

The showdown has been going on for a year since Khan's ouster from power and is now coming to a crescendo.

Khan has challenged his benefactors in the security establishment and political opponents alike, turning the political game on its head. The electoral victories in the by-elections last year only added to his appeal and popularity.

The ruling coalition has fumbled and faltered, battered by its handling of the economy, and sagging public ratings. Its reluctance to go for early elections has been viewed as a sign of weakness by Khan supporters and has only bolstered their morale. The legal drama that has been playing out in the fractured Supreme Court has added to the political turmoil. In such a volatile backdrop, Khan's sudden arrest on corruption charges left his supporters stunned.

But Khan's party might have overplayed its hand. The images of the attacks on the GHQ, the nerve centre of the country's military, and the Lahore Corps Commander's House have rankled the rank and file. The stream of leaked audio and social media videos points to an organized and orchestrated campaign to target state and military institutions. Even though the senior party leadership has distanced itself from the violence, it cannot wash its hands of the consequences. There will be arrests. There will be lengthy legal proceedings.

But it cannot be denied that the military faces a daunting challenge in restoring its reputation and reversing the damage done to its traditional mystique in the wake of recent events. A considerable number of protesters hail from military families and reside in wealthy Defence Housing Authority (DHA) neighbourhoods, and they reject conventional, dynastic politics. It will be a difficult task to regain their loyalty and steer them away from the PTI's narrative. Additionally, it will be equally challenging to counteract the ongoing flow of propaganda and criticism originating from abroad.

Did the architects of 'Project Imran' ever anticipate retired majors and colonels continuously judging and criticizing high-ranking army generals, or that dissidents would publicly reveal the addresses of intelligence officials' residences and safe houses in Islamabad, or incite attacks on military residential compounds in Chaklala or ISI offices in Faisalabad? The current climate is far from normal when rumours of a rift among top military brass or discussions of a 'Colonel's Coup' are casually thrown around.

The political situation in the country has reached uncharted territory, with the ruling coalition banking on the disqualification of Khan from future elections. However, any escalation in violence or prolonged unrest on the streets could result in unforeseen consequences. If Khan is incarcerated for an extended period, it may increase his popularity and sway public opinion further in his favour. The military leadership will find it challenging to maintain its apolitical stance while avoiding having its reputation further hollowed out. For a country already struggling with deepening economic turmoil and unprecedented inflation, additional political unrest will only exacerbate the decline.

Chapter 54

On the Brink

*The danger of civil unrest taking an even
more dangerous violent turn*

Khan has not demonstrated any signs of capitulating. In
his speech soon after he was released from custody after the
Supreme Court granted him bail, Khan increased his rhetorical
intensity. He had an impassioned and irate tone; he was his
usual confrontational self.

He made fun of a general heading the military's media wing
for being too young to understand Khan's importance to the
nation's reputation and standing in the world. Khan reprimanded
and referred to a different general, who oversees the national
accountability bureau, and accused him of attempting to link
him and his wife to the Al-Qadir Trust legal case (Khan and
his wife are accused of granting favours to a powerful real estate
tycoon, Malik Riaz, in return for donations and gifts). Both
deny the charges.

Khan has long since decoded that the military would be
forced to back down by the danger of civil unrest, direct conflict,
and general humiliation. Some in the institution and the civilian
apparatus support him. He will advance with all his strength
and thunder.

Some see parallels in Khan's populism (and his inherent authoritarian streak) with Germany before the Second World War. At that time, the Weimar Republic was severely divided, with both societal and political divisions and economic instability. Adolf Hitler made alliances with some parts of the elite and industrialists. Hitler also ensured that the German military was purged of his opponents and filled with loyalists. This allowed Hitler to consolidate and expand his power.

Khan's constant attack on the army leadership seemed aimed at ensuring that the institution caved into his demand. Many in the institution sympathize with him, considering Imran's political opponents corrupt and inept.

The biggest wild card has been the Supreme Court. Despite divisions within the court, Chief Justice Umar Atta Bandial has faced accusations of bias and favouritism towards Khan. Under his leadership, the court has provided exceptional relief to Khan amidst numerous legal cases. The court's alignment with Khan and its confrontational stance towards the military implies that they perceive their interests to be aligned with Khan's.

Unable to control the judges, the ruling coalition has been forced to finally attempt street agitation. Maulana Fazal-ur-Rehman, the head of the JUI-F religious political party, has been tasked with providing the muscle. Thousands of his stick-wielding supporters are expected to assemble outside the Supreme Court on Monday. The tactic is aimed at pressuring the Bandial-led supreme court bench to desist from initiating contempt proceedings against the government, which has refused to hold provincial elections on 14 May.

The Supreme Court's deadline has already passed. Next week will take Pakistan to the brink as political fighting takes a further violent turn.

A Stark Choice for the Military

The military is under attack from various fronts. Its traditional reputation is damaged, and opponents are rejoicing. The events of 9 May, when PTI protesters attacked military installations, including the GHQ and the Lahore Corps Commander's House, brought embarrassment. The 'myth is broken,' the son of PTI leader Ejaz Chaudhry gleefully claimed. In order to regain prestige, the military commanders will have to move quickly, both on the political and communication fronts.

The military as an institution has a lot of soul-searching to do anyway.

'The entire media apparatus that the military mobilised to delegitimize traditional parties and elevate Khan to office has turned on the military,' as Mosharraf Zaidi, a political commentator, noted.

Authorities are now arresting and actively searching for those involved in acts of arson and vandalism, utilising surveillance footage and other means to identify the culprits.

But the current political turmoil is more of a battle of survival for all the main players involved, and the possibilities of dialogue and reconciliation have diminished with every passing day.

There is a coordinated effort to create controversy around Army Chief Gen. Asim Munir and his command. Various forms of online content, such as vlogs, WhatsApp messages, tweets and TikTok videos, are being used to build pressure and shape public perception regarding Gen. Munir's role. There has been speculation that this cannot happen without inside support. A Pakistani army spokesperson has strongly denied reports of any rift and asserted that the unity of command is intact.

Khan himself accused the army chief of being solely responsible for the current political turmoil during his media interactions with the news media in the Islamabad High Court earlier this week. Khan had initially made ISI internal security wing chief Maj. Gen. Faisal Naseer, a Munir confidante and loyalist, his target.

Now he has thrown the gauntlet straight at Gen. Asim Munir. The army chief has to assert himself now or risk losing authority.

Chapter 55

A Moment of Reckoning for Khan's Political Party

Imran Khan's party jolted by defections

May 2023

Back-to-back defections have rocked Khan's political party. One of the most significant early departures came from Shireen Mazari, the former human rights minister in Imran's cabinet. Mazari, seventy-one, not only announced her resignation from the party but also her retirement from politics altogether. She explained that she wanted to dedicate more time to her children, especially following the recent passing of her husband, as well as attending to her elderly mother. Many people, though, believed that she was being coerced into leaving politics.

After receiving bail from the courts, Mazari experienced a string of re-arrests within a week. The strategy, which PTI described as a mockery of the law, broke her down.

The plight of Mazari also garnered sympathy from many in the media. Witnessing Mazari's downfall was described as a sombre sight by some.

Mazari is a controversial figure known for her combative nature and tendency to promote and relish conspiracy theories, mostly about America. Her tweets have often been scrutinized for disseminating disinformation, propaganda and unfounded allegations. Imran's party provided a suitable platform for her due to these traits.

Following Khan's removal from power last year, Mazari became even more vocal in her criticisms of the United States and the Pakistani military, accusing both of conspiring to remove Imran from office. As a former teacher in the Defence and Strategic Studies Department (DSS) at Quaid-e-Azam University in Islamabad, she has instructed numerous military officers. In recent months, she used DSS terminology to support Imran's confrontation with the establishment, claiming that the balance of power had shifted away from them.

Her announcement to quit politics can be seen as a tactical retreat. At her age, jail time can be extremely uncomfortable.

Another early notable defection was by Fayyaz-ul-Hassan Chohan, a former Punjab provincial information minister. Crude and crass, Chohan was an embarrassment when in office and even more so when out of government; his politics are defined by myopia, xenophobia and fanaticism. He accused Imran of giving him short shrift and criticized the policy of taking on the military establishment. He is one of those politicians who has made their career riding on the back of the Establishment.

Chohan held the position of Punjab provincial information minister in 2020 but was sacked soon from the ministry for making inappropriate comments about religious minorities. He also gained notoriety after his videos with controversial TikTok stars surfaced. His defection is not really a surprise, as he found himself sidelined in the party long ago.

But the steady drip of defections over the past week has dented the morale of Imran's party. These can have a significant impact on the 'electables' (politicians from establishment political families) in Punjab, who are known to sway whichever way the wind is blowing.

Imran and his party members accused the military establishment of forcing these defections—forced divorces, in Imran's words.

However, many people do not miss the irony. Back in 2017–18, the Establishment of that time undertook a similar campaign aimed at fracturing and subduing Nawaz Sharif's party. Despite facing lengthy jail sentences, the senior leaders of Sharif's party displayed more resilience as they remained steadfast.

In contrast, Khan's party is rapidly falling apart.

Fawad Chaudhry, a typically astute politician known for his sharp wit, awkwardly attempted to evade arrest. Video footage of him, visibly exhausted and out of breath as he ran away from the police to the safety of a court, quickly spread across the internet.

More defections are expected in the coming days as pressure mounts on the remaining party members.

The speed with which the party is falling into disarray has shocked and disappointed its supporters, many of whom ignored the state's ham-handed approach in 2017/18. They cheered and rejoiced when Khan's opponents were being hounded and jailed. Today, the circumstances have been reversed.

Pakistan's democracy follows a similar tableau year after year: the script remains the same, but the cast of characters keeps changing.

The events of 9 May, when Khan was crudely arrested by paramilitary troops and triggered violent protests and assaults on military installations, have now led to a significant shift in political momentum against the PTI. Looking back, the party made a misjudgement by assuming that the violence would compel the military to engage in negotiations.

Additionally, some sensationalist YouTubers and journalists who show greater loyalty than necessarily have an impact on the PTI's narrative. In their imaginative realm, fiction seamlessly fits into convenient conspiracy theories, which they constantly modify and revise with each passing day.

Some other self-proclaimed 'revolutionaries' also experienced a harsh dose of reality. Khadija Shah, a businessperson, and the granddaughter of a former army chief, finally surrendered to the authorities after evading capture for several days.

Khadija Shah and her sibling exhibit fervent support for the PTI, and she is accused of inciting violence outside the Lahore Corps Commander House on 9 May. Shah denies instigating violence or attacks on military installations. Before her arrest, her father, Salman Shah, a prominent economist; her husband, from an influential business family; and her brother were briefly detained by the police.

Given their affiliation with the elite of Lahore, many believed that individuals like Shah would never face arrest. Numerous influential figures also advocated on her behalf and attempted to persuade the military high command against her arrest.

However, the top command has chosen to treat Shah's case as a litmus test, using its symbolism to ensure compliance from others within the ranks. If someone of her stature, the granddaughter of a former army chief, and her family can be apprehended in such a manner, others have little chance of evading consequences for their attacks on the military. Shah was finally granted bail in late October.

Chapter 56

Major Shake-Up in Pakistan's Military

High-ranking officers dismissed

June 2023

In a press conference, Maj. Gen. Ahmed Sharif Chaudhry, the director-general ISPR, revealed the implementation of disciplinary measures against several high-ranking military commanders. The army dismissed three senior officers, including a lieutenant general, from their positions, Maj. Gen. Chaudhry said. Additionally, the spokesperson reported that three major generals and seven brigadiers' disciplinary cases were over.

This action taken against a large number of senior officers is unparalleled in recent decades, with the last instance of bulk punishment occurring during a mutiny case several decades ago.

According to top security officials, no evidence points to an internal coup plotted on 9 May. The execution of a coup would have required coordination between the alleged perpetrators and individuals within the GHQ, which was not found. The rumours about three corps commanders teaming up to pressure army chief Gen. Syed Asim Munir on 9 May or a group of generals going to the chairman of the Joint Chiefs of Staff

Committee and urging it to open a dialogue with Khan are unfounded and part of the disinformation campaign, security officials said.

The sacked officers were held accountable for their negligence and failure to act in protecting military installations. Lt Gen. Salman Fayaz Ghani, the former Lahore Corps Commander who has been dismissed, had received instructions to enhance security measures as protesters assembled in Lahore. He opted to permit the mob's unhindered access into the cantonment and instructed the guards to stand down. Lt Gen. Ghani mistakenly believed that the protesters were merely expressing their anger and would disperse after venting themselves.

However, this proved to be a miscalculation, as the protesters not only trespassed on his official residence but also set it ablaze. The general and his family, who were initially offering tea to the mob to calm down, were forced to evacuate hastily from the premises.

Director-general ISPR stressed during the presser that the trial of 102 civilians in military courts will continue, a rebuke and signal to the current Supreme Court proceedings on military trials.

Retired but Active

Several retired generals were actively supporting the 'revival of the project', security officials say. One of the retired generals felt that he still had a role to play if Imran Khan made a successful political comeback. He was also tipped to be the next president, or director-general ISI. Other generals were sympathetic due to several factors: personal liking for the political leader, hatred for conventional political dynasties, and being part of 'the project.'

They proposed a three-pronged strategy, which included:

- *Sustained display of popularity*: Consistently emphasising the leader's popularity and relevance through continuous promotion and messaging.
- *Pressuring top military leadership*: Engaging in verbal attacks on the army chief, director-general ISI, DG C*, and sector commanders of Lahore and Islamabad to create controversy and potentially lead to their removal from their positions.
- *Escalation of conflict*: Engaging in violent confrontations, protests, and attacks on military installations to compel the senior military leadership to respond. The inclusion of casualties would have heightened the impact of the campaign.

The Cost of Constant Brinksmanship

Once considered a stronghold of support, the military's backing played a significant role in Khan's ascension to power in 2018. His popularity among military families, who were disenchanted with the corruption of previous civilian governments, was evident as they actively participated in his political rallies.

Even after senior generals withdrew their support in 2021, Khan maintained considerable backing from the military community, particularly veterans. However, the tide turned after 9 May 2023 riots, and many veterans have distanced themselves from Khan.

Retired Brigadier Ashfaq Hassan, who was once a staunch supporter, expressed his disillusionment, stating that Khan is

---

* Refers to an important position in the ISI, held by a major general. It is generally referred to as DG counterintelligence (DG C or DG CI) and primarily deals with local politics. Critics say the position holder influences domestic politics, often resulting in the making or breaking of political parties or the rise and fall of politicians.

now viewed as an enemy due to his hostile campaign against the army and its leadership.

Observers note that Khan's party was initially pro-establishment, formed to challenge the dominance of political dynasties. It consisted of the urban middle class, military elites and the business community, all of whom desired stability through military involvement in politics.

Despite initial loyalty, disillusionment grew among party members following Khan's removal from power last year, exacerbated by the events of 9 May and the subsequent crackdown. Muhammad Zubair, a former governor of Sindh province, explained that the defections stem from a lack of conviction in the cause and an inability to withstand the mounting pressure.

The effects of the crackdown and defections are apparent, with Khan's residence in Lahore now appearing desolate. The number of supporters visiting has dwindled, leaving him isolated and facing a multitude of legal cases.

His persistent antagonistic approach towards the army chief and top generals, even after their initial overtures of support, surprised many, considering the upcoming elections and his favourable standing in surveys.

Khan's failure to nurture a positive relationship with the new chief and his unwarranted attacks on the military, instead of focusing on the ruling coalition's mismanagement of the economy, raised eyebrows, Zubair noted.

This strained dynamic provided an opportunity for those waiting to strike back, ultimately trapping Khan in a precarious position.

Chapter 57

Fallout

August 2023

On 5 August 2023, Imran Khan finally found himself incarcerated after a trial court convicted him of misusing state gifts and misrepresenting his assets. Compared to the uproar of 9 May, the public's reaction this time was noticeably restrained and muted. This could be largely attributed to the aftermath of 9 May, marked by the detentions of influential figures of Khan's political party, internal party upheavals after an array of defections, and the stringent crackdown.

Soon after, Khan was relegated to Attock's notoriously grim district jail. Housed in a modest 9x11 cell, his initial nights, as described by his associates, were battles against relentless mosquitoes and bugs. His lawyers also claimed that rainwater had seeped into the prison cell. While there were loud grumblings, questioning the trial's impartiality, his legal team geared up for an appeal and lobbied for his transfer to Adiala Jail in Rawalpindi, known for comparatively better accommodations for political prisoners.

The political arena buzzed. Imran's adversaries revelled in the irony, recalling his past provocations towards the PML–N and PPP leadership and his vows to strip jail privileges, now echoed endlessly across media platforms.

In a conversation with me soon after the arrest, Information Minister Marriyum Aurangzeb cautioned against hasty parallels. She underscored the legality of Khan's arrest and his evasive manoeuvres during the trial. Arguing against allegations of political vendetta, she highlighted the government's restraint, contrasting Imran's approach to the law with Nawaz Sharif's approach to appearing before the courts of law after the Panama Papers scandal. The minister was particularly vocal about Khan's diversionary tactics since his removal from power and debunked theories linking his arrest to the forthcoming elections. She emphasized the myriad legal charges against him and concluded with a stern proclamation: 'The time is up.'

Yet the narrative is multifaceted and complicated.

Khan's loyalists fervently view the events as orchestrated to shatter their leader's spirit. Despite his trials, they proclaim his unwavering mass appeal and eagerly anticipate his eventual release. But Khan's looming political hiatus, especially from the impending General Election, casts a dark pall over his prospective resurgence.

Still, Khan's enduring influence cannot be denied. His absence from future polls might not erase his political legacy. Pakistan's treacherous political history reminds us that sidelining a leader does not always dissolve their foundational support.

The depth of this backing, especially prominent among the Pakistani diaspora, however, awaits its tangible manifestation. The already fragmented political scene is poised for further decline and deterioration. A considerable segment of the Khan following now finds itself down a cul-de-sac, leaving them oblivious to the repercussions of their incendiary rhetoric and tactics of segregation. Consequently, societal chasms are widening.

Such a tainted political environment is bound to cast long shadows.

While Imran languished in jail, preparations were already afoot for a new political order, sidelining him in the 2023–2024 electoral dance. On 8 August, the country's election commission disqualified Imran for five years.

A contentious legal battle will now ensue as Khan tries to get the conviction overturned and fight the array of legal challenges thrown at him. With the ruling coalition dissolving the National Assembly in the second week of August 2023, creating the path for an interim arrangement, strong speculations are already circulating within political circles regarding the possibility of an extended interim government setup.

The 'hybrid rule' is now expected to change and alter its composition. There are already signs that a new assertive approach is being adopted by the military establishment.

Khan has successfully motivated people who were earlier averse to challenging the military to openly question and criticize the security establishment's meddling in politics. The Pakistani military faces a daunting challenge in winning the hearts and minds of a large section of the population, which, not too long ago, regarded it as the saviour and deliverer.

General Syed Asim Munir, the Pakistani army chief, has taken on this challenge and hopes to facilitate foreign investment worth billions of dollars into the country through a mix of improvement in the country's agricultural sector and easing up of business opportunities, especially in the country's mining and energy sectors. Critics will view these developments as yet another encroachment of the military into the civilian sphere while the military will defend its actions as necessitated by the need to stabilize the economy, essential for the country's survival and stability.

The ruling coalition that governed from April 2022 until August 2023, led by Prime Minister Shehbaz Sharif, has come under criticism for failing to uphold the sanctity of the parliament and willingly assisting and enabling the curtailing of civil liberties as attempts were made to remove Imran from the electoral field.

Sharif dismisses these concerns, asserting instead that it was not an easy job to head a disparate coalition that confronted a tanking economy, climate change calamities in the form of the worst floods, and the potent political challenge posed by Imran and his allies in the judiciary.

On 14 August 2023, as the country celebrated its Seventy-Sixth Independence Day, Anwaar-ul Haq Kakar, an ethnic Pashtun senator, hailing from Balochistan, took oath as the caretaker prime minister. Kakar, notably younger than his predecessors in the role of caretaker prime minister, is a media-savvy political activist who has contacts across the political spectrum. But his biggest strength has been his close ties with the Establishment. His sudden nomination was seen as having been pushed and stamped by the powerful quarters and left no doubt that the military was once again firmly back in the saddle.

In August 2023, the American news website Intercept controversially released the Cipher, a diplomatic memo sent by the Pakistani US ambassador to the foreign office in Islamabad last year.[*]

Just before his removal from power in 2022 through a no-confidence vote in the parliament, Imran had asserted that the US had plotted to remove him.[**] He alleged that a diplomatic cable had conveyed a warning about his removal. Intercept, the news website, staunchly asserted that an official of the Pakistani military was the source of the leak.

---

[*] Ryan Grim and Murtaza Hussain, 'Secret Pakistan Cable Documents U.S. Pressure to Remove Imran Khan,' *Intercept*, 9 August 2023, https://theintercept.com/2023/08/09/imran-khan-pakistan-cypher-ukraine-russia/, accessed on 19 March 2024.

[**] Imran has made this accusation on a number of times since his April 2022 ouster and its well documented. PTI, 'Imran Khan Blames Biden Administration Toppling His Government Through Conspiracy', *Indian Express*, 2 May 2022, https://indianexpress.com/article/pakistan/imran-khan-biden-government-conspiracy-7898421/), accessed on 19 March 2024.

Accepting this claim at face value is challenging, especially considering the journalists associated with the website's forceful and almost hysterical insistence on the source's authenticity. My tweet that the source was 'likely' to be from within Khan's party kicked up a storm on X, the social-media platform formerly known as Twitter. The coordinated social-media attack against me by the journalists associated with the Intercept and PTI raised suspicions about the real intent.[*]

Although the news website admitted to being unable to independently verify the Cipher's contents, they still chose to publish it—a move that lacks the integrity expected from reputable news outlets.

The unauthenticated cipher's contents revealed a confrontational exchange between two diplomats, further confirming my longstanding position that the US and Khan government's relations were deeply strained. This had been previously reported, as detailed in this book's 'The Cipher Mystery' chapter. The publication of the secret Cipher had some implications. Only one unaccounted copy existed, and Imran himself acknowledged in an interview with a local news television network that he had somehow lost or misplaced it. The Pakistani government promptly reacted by promising an inquiry into any potential breach of national security.

For PTI supporters, however, the exchange between American and Pakistani diplomats validated their belief in a foreign conspiracy to remove Imran from power. Nevertheless, this episode further exacerbated an already strained and tense relationship between Khan and the country's security establishment.

Historically in the country, the military and civilians have always been two separate political entities in continual contention. Civilian politicians, when not in power, often fuel

---

[*] Ryan Grim's (*Intercept*) post on X, https://x.com/ryangrim/status/168934228075311 9232?s=46&t=y5hgy 3Brlj2OtJqOiPE_dw

anti-establishment rhetoric, yet paradoxically seek alliances with the establishment to overcome their civilian adversaries. This trend has become increasingly foreseeable.

I vividly recall one evening in October 2011 when I met Khan at his Islamabad mansion, picturesquely overlooking the hills, just a day prior to his mammoth Lahore political rally, a declaration that he had finally arrived as a political force to be reckoned with.

Those were the initial heady days for Khan, and they were full of optimism and excitement for his followers; his appeal stretching from the urban middle class to the tribal regions of the country.

Khan exuded energy as we sat in his drawing room, its walls adorned with his glamorous pictures from over the years. His dog played around his legs on the tiled floor. His house had a quiet feel, devoid of the usual swarm of loyalists, supplicants, or hopeful politicians that had become commonplace in the following years. 'Nobody can stop the revolution,' he said with his trademark conviction as he dismissed his rival political leaders as part of the rot afflicting the country.

Even at that time, critics warned that Khan's politics were vague and contradictory and relied just on his charisma. But in the subsequent years, as he inched closer to power, helped by the powerful establishment, there was immense hope and expectation in the country about his promise for social justice and change.

But those promises and hopes came to nought as his years in power saw him descend into the same spiral that consumed his political rivals. His erstwhile harmonious alliance with the establishment, which for a brief while reshaped the nation's power dynamics, now lies fractured. In the ensuing political tumult since his 2022 ouster, Imran's effort to take on the security establishment took the form of an all-out confrontational policy.

The fallout appeared complete.

Chapter 58

Bomb, Bulldoze and Destroy

The new military strategy

By the end of September 2023, Imran Khan had been relocated to Adiala Prison, a high-security facility in Rawalpindi, adjacent to the capital. This prison has previously housed several former prime ministers, and during his term as prime minister, Khan wanted to remove the air-conditioner and television from his nemesis Sharif's prison cell during his time of incarceration. Khan received a bicycle and a television set restricted to state-run news channels for his use.

Meanwhile, the military establishment formulated a strategy dubbed 'Bomb, Bulldoze, Destroy,' or BDD, essentially targeting illegal economic activities to rejuvenate the struggling economy. In September, authorities conducted a broad crackdown on foreign currency, primarily the US dollar, smuggling, resulting in a substantial appreciation of the local currency.

'The law enforcement agencies and other government bodies will persist in their vigorous actions against a range of illegal activities to prevent resource theft and the economic damages the country incurs from these activities,' the military's media wing reported, quoting Army Chief Gen. Munir in a statement on 5 October 2023. In the same month, Pakistani authorities also announced a new policy to deport illegal aliens on its soil, primarily Afghans, citing security concerns. The move strained Pakistan's ties with the Afghan Taliban, which publicly criticized the new policy. But the security officials forcibly went ahead with the plan to deport Afghans living on Pakistani soil without proper documentation.

The BDD strategy of using relentless force seemed to permeate into the political arena as well, many observers noted, reflecting in the harsh crackdown on the supporters of Pakistan Tehreek-e-Insaf. Some analysts expressed concern that a political strategy consisting solely of punitive measures, without incentives, would fail to produce favourable outcomes.

As Khan remained behind bars, a severe crackdown on his party's leaders and supporters persisted, notably in Punjab. In these mostly late-night raids, houses were forcibly entered, furniture was destroyed, crockery was shattered, and women were manhandled as the police searched for their targets, actions that rights activists condemned as mere intimidation and harassment. Khan's legal proceedings were now conducted within Adiala Prison, creating an expectation that his convictions would demoralize his supporters.

In November, the Election Commission of Pakistan announced that the next elections would be held on 8 February 2024. Since the dissolution of parliament on 9 August, an interim setup has been in charge. The elections were scheduled to occur within ninety days following the dissolution of parliament. However, the Electoral Commission of Pakistan (ECP) held that a delay was necessary to adjust constituency boundaries in light of the most recent census data.

According to the constitution, elections can only proceed after the redrawing of constituencies to reflect the latest census figures, a task the ECP stated would require a minimum of four months to complete.

The run-up to the election remained laden with uncertainty and controversy, as many felt that the enduring popularity of Khan could lead to an even further delay.

However, security officials and political rivals of Khan remained sanguine that the harsh police crackdown had battered the pro-Khan crowd so much that it would not come out to vote. The voters in Pakistan, especially in Punjab, had a history of choosing the side that seemed to have the support of the establishment, and Khan was clearly out of favour.

Khan's supporters asserted that the returning officers rejected the nomination papers of a sizable number of PTI candidates in December 2023 as a ruse to deny the party a level playing field. The candidates had to turn to the high courts for a legal remedy.

As these controversies churned, many were left questioning whether the 8 February elections would plunge the country into yet another round of political turmoil or strife. Some people even advocated for a continuation of the caretaker setup, pointing out that the interim arrangement handled the economy in a better manner than the political coalitions.

Just under a month before the elections, a senior civilian official told me in a detailed background discussion that there would not be any delay in the polls as Senate elections were also due by March to select its new members. He said that most of the rejected nominations of PTI candidates would be overturned, but stressed that those involved in the 9 May 2023, riots would not be allowed to contest.

The official also noted that the stakeholders felt that Khan and his supporters, due to the crackdown, lacked the power and strength to disrupt the system; the biggest challenge to the establishment came on 9 May, when a large number of military installations were targeted by Khan's supporters, incensed over his arrest. Now, most of them were paying a heavy price, either in the form of military trials or removal from the electoral field. Khan remained popular but could only extricate himself after a deal with the Establishment, which seemed distant.

The official said that the army chief, General Munir, had an almost 'messianic zeal and desire' to rectify the economy. The Special Investment Facilitation Council (SIFC), which had been created in June 2023 under the army chief's vision, was to continue even after the new government took charge after the elections.

The SIFC envisioned transforming the economic approach from debt-driven to investment-driven. 'As a "Single Window" platform, it stands to optimize horizontal-vertical synergy, harmonize diverse stakeholders, ensure ease of doing business, and help remove barriers', reads an introduction to the SIFC on its official website.

One lingering question remained: would Nawaz Sharif, should he become prime minister after the elections, be comfortable with such an arrangement? After all, Sharif had previously championed civilian supremacy and sought the final say in decision-making.

Sharif's party, however, remained optimistic and upbeat. Its leaders felt that power was just inches away.

The new year 2024 started with a wave of legal warfare unleashed on Khan. He was convicted and sentenced to ten years in January in the 'cipher case,' in which Khan accused the US of trying to oust him based on a secret diplomatic cable. Subsequently, he shared details, violating secrecy laws, which led to his conviction. Khan was also convicted and handed a fourteen-year prison term in the 'Tosha Khan Case', which alleged that he sold state gifts for-profit and failed to disclose them to the election authorities. Khan and his wife were also sentenced to seven years for violating the law by marrying before the passage of the prescribed three-month '*iddah*' period after Khan's wife's previous divorce.

The speedy convictions were unprecedented and left many shocked. The judges seemed to be in a rush to convict Khan, holding the court proceedings for even eleven to fourteen hours a day as they tried to conclude the cases before 8 February the polling day.

The Election Commission also stripped Khan's political party of its iconic election symbol, the cricket bat. This action—critics and Khan's party said—was intended to create confusion among Khan's voters on election day, as each candidate would now contest as an independent candidate and would then be assigned a different election symbol.

On 4 January 2024, the incarcerated Khan wrote an article in the *Economist*, the British weekly, on invitation. The article, not surprisingly, went viral, and the former prime minister took shots at his two targets: General Bajwa and America. Khan reiterated his claims that the Pakistani establishment 'engineered' his ouster under American pressure because he pursued an independent foreign policy and opposition to the US military bases. He also alleged that General Bajwa influenced his political allies and parliamentary members via security agencies to facilitate the April 2022 no-confidence vote. Khan also claimed that the 9 May 2023, riots and attacks on military installations were a 'false flag operation'.[*]

Meanwhile, on 8 January 2024, the Supreme Court overturned the lifetime disqualification for politicians with past

---

[*] 'Imran Khan Warns that Pakistan's Election Could Be a Farce', *Economist*, 4 January 2024, https://www.economist.com/by-invitation/2024/01/04/imran-khan-warns-that-pakistans-election-could-be-a-farce.

convictions, paving the way for Nawaz Sharif to contest the elections.

Khan's adversaries shrugged off his political comeback as nearly impossible, attributing his popularity solely to social media. They argued that Khan was only popular on X (formerly Twitter), TikTok—the app known for its short videos—and other social media platforms, lacking a tangible presence and the necessary political infrastructure to mobilize voters on election day. Consequently, Khan's party was not anticipated to secure more than forty seats in the forthcoming elections.

Many political analysts contended that Khan had miscalculated the military's response to his constant agitation. While they acknowledged that Khan's support and popularity had swelled, the military's retribution would ensure he remained out of power.

Some politicians, like Mustafa Nawaz Khokar, a former senator who was contesting as an independent from Islamabad, held the view that the whole electoral process lacked credibility, and people generally seemed disinterested due to the feeling that the military held the final word.[*] 'All political parties have accepted it,' Khokhar said in an interview at his Islamabad residence just days before the elections.

'Even when Imran Khan is given a deal, he will happily accept it,' Khokar speculated with a dour look, puffing a cigarette.

Zafarullah Khan, an Islamabad-based constitutional expert and political analyst, however, warned that the conflict between the army and Khan had now spilled on to the street.

He noted that a new class had emerged in the country: the urban and semi-urban population, many of whom had earned a lot of money after going abroad. They were no longer reliant on the state's patronage. They were no longer reliant

---

[*] Interview with me in Islamabad on 25 January 2024.

on government schools. They were no longer reliant on public hospitals. This educated, mostly urban class, he said, was upset that things were not improving for the better in the country. They were unwilling to accept the dynastic political families. They were asking for respect. Khan embodied that sentiment. Despite the crackdown, this urban, semi-urban middle-class was not budging. Khan had also tapped into the vast swath of the poor and the illiterate, giving them a heady mix of religion, populism, and nationalism.

'It will not be a walkover for PML–N or the PPP,' Zafarullah predicted.[*]

---

[*] Interview with me in Islamabad.

Chapter 59

Surprise, Surprise

*Imran Khan scores a stunning
victory on election day*

February 2024

8 February dealt a stunning blow to Khan's political opponents
and the military, leaving them shocked. All the pre-poll
predictions fell flat. Khan's independent candidates scored major
upsets. Sharif's party failed to get the easy win it anticipated.

On the polling day, the authorities shut down mobile phone
services across the country, citing security threats. But the move
was seen as yet another attempt to thwart Khan supporters from
mobilizing and casting votes. But despite a months-long police
crackdown and quick convictions aimed at discouraging Khan's
supporters, they remained undeterred, organizing efficiently
and cleverly through WhatsApp and Facebook on the polling
day to ensure they knew precisely who to vote for. This was
especially crucial in Punjab, the election's main battleground,
where the PML–N's campaign had failed to gain momentum.

Prior to the polling day, concerns were already growing
among PML–N political party leadership about Nawaz Sharif's
relatively modest rally turnouts, ranging from 10,000 to 15,000

attendees. Yet there was a sense of complacency, bolstered by the belief that the army's support guaranteed victory.

After polling concluded on 8 February, the scene at the PML–N headquarters in Lahore's historic Model Town neighbourhood was one of initial confidence, with party leaders and supporters gathering in anticipation of their success. The setup included just a single television, which initially received scant attention as the room buzzed with congratulatory exchanges and the serving of dinner.

However, the atmosphere shifted dramatically as the results started to pour in later in the evening, indicating a surprising trend of victories for Khan and losses for Nawaz's close stalwarts. The disbelief among the PML–N ranks was palpable. In a sudden, quiet, and stunned departure, Nawaz and his daughter Maryam, the political heiress, slipped away from the gathering, a clear sign of their deflation in the face of an unforeseen electoral shift.

Khan's supporters were jubilant.

But by midnight, the results had slowed down. And by the next day, several winners of the previous night were declared losers. And many the losers turned into winners overnight.

Khan's supporters were now incensed and enraged.

They quickly pointed to rigging. They flashed the election results compiled on Form 45, also known as the 'Result of the Count' form. Accusations were levelled against the election authorities for altering the final results on Form 47, which records provisional results within a constituency, including the total votes cast, a candidate-wise breakdown of votes, and the number of votes cancelled or rejected. Form 47 is compiled from the results reported on Form 45s. Once all votes are counted, Forms 48 and 49 are issued to publish the complete and final vote counts, serving as the official declarations of the election outcomes.

These documents became the focal point of the controversy surrounding the election results in Pakistan, as Khan supporters claimed that a deliberate attempt had been made to manipulate the results.

As the controversy over the results in dozens of constituencies swirled, the Election Commission was conspicuously slow to release the final results.

The outcome of the 8 February elections, nonetheless, presented a fragmented political landscape as no political party managed to secure a majority. The independents, mostly affiliated with Khan, secured 101 seats, according to the initial vote count. Khan's supporters, on the other hand, claimed that they had actually won 180 seats. Sharif's party got seventy-five seats. The Pakistan People's Party managed fifty-four seats.

If the country was looking for stability after the contentious polls, it was not to be. The military establishment's plan of isolating and sidelining Khan was also in disarray. The electoral result was also a stinging rebuke to the military's 9 May narrative, as most of the candidates facing cases related to 9 May won their seats.

In Adiala Prison, Khan basked in his success. He knew he had gained even more political power, the mandate given by his followers was enough to upset the political equation his adversaries wanted to write. All pre-election predictions and notions had been thrown out the window.

Subsequently, Khan refused to make an alliance with other political parties, even though a ruling coalition with the PPP would have ensured immediate power. His supporters said they would try to form a government without the political actors that played a part in his April 2022 ouster from the government.

Sharif withdrew his bid to become prime minister, which he wanted to accomplish for the fourth time, in shock over the poor poll results. His younger brother, Shehbaz, was entrusted with forming a ruling coalition and leading it in a reprise of the 2022 shaky, ruling alliance post-Khan's ouster. But everyone knew that this was a crown of barbed wire. Bilawal Bhutto

Zardari, the co-chairman of the PPP, was reluctant to become part of the cabinet, anticipating that the incoming government would be forced to take an array of drastic economic measures, resulting in public approval and popularity plummeting sharply. Taking the reins of government was, politically, a kiss of death.

Meanwhile, Khan's loyalists also vowed to form the government, both in KP province and in Islamabad.

The incoming government faces an uphill—some would say impossible—task.

The next government will be constantly hounded by questions about legitimacy and credibility, and the perennial challenges of the economy and security will loom large. The risk of economic default was precariously sidestepped in 2023, but the dependence on foreign aid means a rocky path ahead. There are no solutions available to fix the economy without further inflicting pain on an already emaciated public. The public is still reeling from the pain of austerity measures. Inflation and skyrocketing utility bills remain a key concern.

At the same time, there is an uptick in terrorist attacks, with 2023 marking the deadliest year in six years. The aftermath of the catastrophic 2022 floods, a reminder of climate change that affected millions, poses another urgent concern for effective governance. And there is no respite available on the foreign policy front. The western flank is now riddled with tensions; the Afghan Taliban are disgruntled; and the brief cross-border skirmish with Iran has added a new layer to security challenges. The eastern front has been quiet for some time, but yet another Modi win in the upcoming Indian elections can also lead to a more jingoistic approach from the archival.

Khan pulled off an electoral success that many thought was impossible. There is a prevailing sentiment in the country that his return to power is inevitable. Despite employing various tactics in its traditional, mostly successful playbook, the military was unable to secure Khan's defeat in the 8 February elections. With a young demographic poised to play a decisive role in the next three elections, Khan has successfully imbued them with an anti-establishment sentiment. The young are loudly questioning the meddling of the military in politics. Khan deftly turned the 8 February election into a referendum on him versus the military. He has successfully carved himself into the public imagination as the sole figure taking on the corrupt politicians and a hegemonic military.

The powerful generals have always thought of themselves and the army as the real custodians of the country and the arbiters of power. But even within this powerful clique, there was a reckoning that the traditional prestige of the institution had been greatly dented. Following the election results, some voices within the institution expressed concerns that its legitimacy was rapidly diminishing, advocating for a change in direction. They argued that a hybrid model of governance was unsustainable and called for the acceptance of Khan's mandate. But the top brass appeared to be pushing ahead for a setup post-election that ensured Khan's party did not have power in the centre.

On 3 March, Shehbaz Sharif was elected as the prime minister of the country, easily managing a majority in the national assembly.

In November 2025, General Munir, the current Pakistani army chief's term will finish, leading to either an extension in his tenure, as often has been the case in the country's history, or a new appointment. A new army chief might opt for reconciliation with Khan or continue Munir's policies. But such outcomes are unpredictable at present. What is clear is that the country will continue on its tumultuous trajectory, marked by deep-seated civil–military imbalance, political divisions, discord and power struggles.

Acknowledgements

My unwavering gratitude is reserved for my parents, Saeeda Khan and Masood Ahmed Chaudhry. Their love and blessings have been the compass guiding my journey. Ayesha Hayat Khan, my wife, remains my anchor and guiding light. My daughter, Aysel, infuses our lives with immeasurable joy. They have been very patient with my work commitments, which often clash with our family moments.

Scan QR code to access the
Penguin Random House India website